MAYLAND COMMUNITY COLLEGE - LRC

3 3270 00034 6452

QH
54.5
.N3
2000

LEARNING RESOURCES CENTER
MAYLAND COMMUNITY COLLEGE
PO BOX 547
SPRUCE PINE, NC 28777

D1298031

21.95

Nature
Theme-A-Saurus

The Great Big Book of Nature Units

DATE DUE

GAYLORD   PRINTED IN U.S.A.

Edited by GAYLE BITTINGER

Illustrated by MARILYNN BARR

Totline® Publications
A Division of Frank Schaffer Publications, Inc.
Torrance, California

Totline® Publications would especially like to thank the following child-care professionals for their contributions that were used in this book: Ruth Cox Anderson, Pat Beck, Nancy Nason Biddinger, John M. Bittinger, Sue Brown, Marie Cecchini, Patty Claycomb, Sharon Clendenen, Kathleen Cubley, Cindy Dingwall, Ann-Marie Donovan, Adele Engelbracht, Barbara B. Fleisher, Nancy H. Giles, Judy Hall, Mildred Hoffman, Colraine Pettipaw Hunley, Debra Lindahl, Elizabeth McKinnon, Judith McNitt, Margo S. Miller, Susan A. Miller, Susan M. Paprocki, Susan Peters, Lois E. Putnam, Bev Qualheim, Polly Reedy, Sue Schliecker, Betty Silkunas, Carla C. Skjong, Judy Slenker, Kathleen Soman, Colleen Stockton, Heather Tekavec, Diane Thom, Martha Thomas, Margaret Timmons, Becky Valenick, Kathie Vogel, Elizabeth Vollrath, Kristine Wagoner, Cynthia Walters, Saundra Winnett, Bonnie Woodard, and Deborah Zumbar.

Managing Editor: Mina McMullin
Editor: Gayle Bittinger
Contributing Editors: Kathy Zaun, Jean Warren
Editorial Assistant: Mary Newmaster
Graphic Designer (Interior): Jill Kaufman
Graphic Designer (Cover): Brenda Mann Harrison
Cover Illustration: Marilynn Barr
Production Manager: Janie Schmidt

Copyright © 2000 by Totline® Publications. All rights reserved. Except for reproducing the pattern pages for noncommercial use or for including brief quotations in a review, no part of this book may be reproduced in any form without the written consent of the publisher.

Theme-A-Saurus® is a registered trademark of Warren Publishing House, Inc.

ISBN: 1-57029-263-9

Published by Totline® Publications
A Division of Frank Schaffer Publications
23740 Hawthorne Blvd.
Torrance, CA 90505

Introduction

Children of all ages delight in the wonder of the world around them. Plants, animals, rain, rocks, and water lead them to exciting discoveries about their environment. *Nature Theme-A-Saurus* is a collection of activities designed to capture your children's interest in nature. These stimulating activities can be used to teach a variety of concepts. The book is divided into five broad chapters: seasons, animals, plants and food, weather, and earth and sky. Each chapter contains a wonderful array of topics.

The ideas in this book will let you follow your children's lead as they explore the world around them. They can become a springboard for other experiences you may want to introduce the children to. For example, a trip to the zoo can be followed up with zoo animal activities and songs. An unexpected collection of rocks can lead to many rock explorations.

As with all Totline® books, the activities in *Nature Theme-A-Saurus* are simple, fun, age-appropriate, and involve the use of readily available materials. The many songs and rhymes are ones your children will want to sing and say over and over again. Plus, each chapter includes learning patterns to save you time.

Look to nature and *Nature Theme-A-Saurus* to inspire you and your children for all kinds of new and expanded learning opportunities. Enjoy your learning explorations together!

Contents

Seasons

Fall

Leaf Mural

Let your children help you collect an assortment of fall leaves. Draw a large, bare tree shape on a sheet of butcher paper. Spread the butcher paper on the floor or on a table. Let your children glue the leaves they collected all over the paper to create a Leaf Mural. Allow the glue to dry before hanging up the mural.

Leaf Hair

Set out a basket of dry fall leaves. Give each of your children a sheet of construction paper. Help each child draw a face shape on his or her paper. Show the children how to glue the leaves around their face shapes to make "hair." Let them make as many faces as they wish.

Leaf Creatures

For each of your children, glue a large dried leaf on a sheet of construction paper. Give each child one of the papers and some markers. Let the children use the markers to turn their leaves into "creatures" by drawing on arms, legs, faces, and other features. Have extra sheets ready for children who would like to make Leaf Creature families.

Pumpkin Faces

Prepare a batch of orange modeling dough (use your own recipe or follow the one below). Give each of your children a handful of the orange dough and a plastic lid (from a coffee can, whipped topping container, or other similar container). Have the children press the dough into their lids and smooth it out. Set out popcorn kernels. Let them use the kernels to create faces on their orange dough "pumpkins."

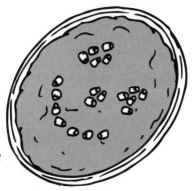

Orange Modeling Dough

Mix together 1 cup flour, ½ cup salt, 6 to 7 tablespoons water, 1 tablespoon vegetable oil. To color the dough, stir in a few drops of red and yellow food coloring. Or, for a more brilliant color, sprinkle on a little orange tempera paint powder and mix well. Makes enough for three to four children.

Pumpkin Printing

If you have a carved pumpkin in your room, instead of discarding it after Halloween, use it for print-making first. Cut the pumpkin into chunks. Give each of your children a piece. Show them how to use a nail to carve designs on the insides of their pumpkin pieces. When they are finished, have them press the carved sides of their pumpkin pieces first on ink pads and then on sheets of construction paper to make pumpkin prints.

Paper Bag Pumpkins

Collect brown paper bags in various sizes. Set out sheets of newspaper and the paper bags. Let each of your children choose one of the paper bags and open it up. Show the children how to crumple up sheets of newspaper and stuff them in their paper bags. When the bags are full, tie each one closed with a piece of yarn. Let your children paint their bags to look like pumpkins. Allow the paint to dry before placing the pumpkins all around your room.

Extension: To create a pumpkin patch, arrange the pumpkins in a space on the floor and tie them together with green yarn "vines." Attach green paper leaves to complete your pumpkin patch.

Fall

Nutshell Collages

Fall is a great time to collect nutshells. Let your children (if they are three or older) crack and eat nuts for a snack, saving the shells for this activity. After the shells have been collected, ask your children to think of ways to break them into smaller pieces. Let them try a few of their ideas. When you have small pieces of nutshells, set out sheets of lightweight cardboard or other sturdy paper, small bowls of glue, and brushes. Let your children brush glue on their papers and then arrange the nutshell pieces on them. Encourage them to notice all the different colors of brown they see.

Hint: Ask your children's families to save nutshells, too.

Nut Boats

To make Nut Boats, you will need half of a walnut shell for each of your children. In addition, each boat requires a small amount of modeling dough, a round toothpick for a mast, and a small square of construction paper for a sail. Let each child decorate his or her sail with crayons or markers. Help the children thread their sails on their toothpicks. Show them how to put the modeling dough inside their shell halves and stick the toothpick mast and paper sail in the dough. Set out a pan or tub of water. Let your children sail their boats on the water.

Apple Man Puppet

Stick whole cloves into the side of an apple to make two eyes, a nose, and a mouth. Stick toothpicks on either side of the face to make arms. Attach carrot curls with toothpicks for hair, if desired. Let your children take turns making up stories about Apple Man's adventures. Record their stories on tape so they can listen to them again later. Write each child's response on paper and let him or her illustrate the story.

Do You Know the Apple Man?

Sing the song below with your children. Let them take turns holding the Apple Man puppet from the activity described above while they make up additional verses about him and his adventures.

Sung to: "The Muffin Man"

Oh, do you know the Apple Man,
The Apple Man, the Apple Man?
Oh, do you know the Apple Man
Who likes to play with me?

Oh, he has a great big smile,
A great big smile, a great big smile.
Oh, he has a great big smile
And likes to play with me.

Jean Warren

Fall

Apple Sort

Have your children sort different colored real or cardboard apples into baskets. Let them count how many red, green, and yellow apples are in each basket. Which color has the most apples? Which one has the least? Ask your children to arrange each group of apples by size, from the largest to the smallest.

Apple Numbers

Make a felt apple tree and ten felt apples for your flannelboard. Number the apples from 1 to 10. Let each of your children in turn choose an apple, identify the number on it, and place the apple on the tree. When all the apples are on the tree, count them as a group.

Apple Recall

At group time, place five to eight apples in front of your children. Have them count the apples. Ask them to close their eyes while you remove some of the apples. Help them figure out how many apples are gone. Repeat several times with different numbers of apples.

How Many Leaves?

Place several leaves in a see-through container such as a glass jar or a clear-plastic bag. Ask your children to estimate how many leaves are inside. Then take out the leaves and count them together. Were their guesses too high or too low? Place a different number of leaves in the container and have the children guess and count again. The more your children practice this, the better they will get at estimating.

Ring Around the Leaves

Take your children outside and have them make a big pile of leaves. Then let them hold hands and walk around their leaf pile as you sing the song below together. When you get to the third line, have the children stop and toss handfuls of leaves up into the air.

Sung to: "Ring Around the Rosie"

Ring around the fall leaves,

Lots and lots of fall leaves.

Leaves . . . Leaves . . .

They all fall down!

Lois E. Putnam

Fall

Harvesting Movements

Ask your children to climb an imaginary ladder and use their hands to pick fruit such as apples, oranges, and cherries. Next, have the harvesters climb down from their ladders and dig in the dirt with their hands to gather potatoes and pull carrots. Let your children name other fruits and vegetables for everyone to "harvest."

Vegetable Soup

After your children have harvested all their fruits and vegetables as described in the Harvesting Movements activity above, ask them to help make some Vegetable Soup. Have everyone stand around an imaginary soup pot, stirring as they add the vegetables. As they stir, sing the song below. Continue with additional verses about other vegetables your children would like to add to the soup. Finish with the final verse as you pretend to serve a bowl of soup to each child. Let them "eat" the delicious soup they made together.

Sung to: "The Farmer in the Dell"

The soup is boiling up,
The soup is boiling up.
Stir slow, around we go,
The soup is boiling up.

Now we add some carrots,
Now we add some carrots.
Stir slow, around we go,
Now we add some carrots.

The soup is ready now,
The soup is ready now.
Stir slow, around we go,
The soup is ready now.

Jean Warren

Applesauce

Quarter, core, and peel 3 to 4 apples. Cut the apple quarters in half and put them in a saucepan. Add ½ cup water and sprinkle on ½ teaspoon of cinnamon. Cover and simmer until tender, about 20 minutes. Let your children help you mash the apples with a potato masher. Cool and serve. Makes 6 small servings.

Apple Rings

Core several apples. Fill the hollowed out centers with peanut butter. Slice the apples into ½-inch thick "rings." Serve. Your children will love the unusual shape and the tasty peanut butter addition.

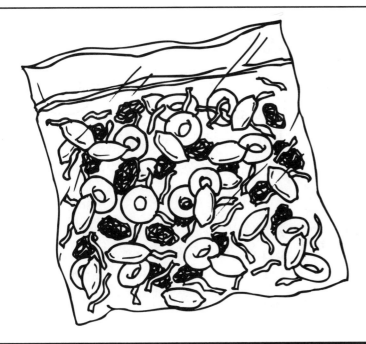

Nutty Trail Mix

Help your children crack their own nuts for this special snack mix. Set out bowls of the shelled nuts, shredded coconut, O-shaped cereal, and raisins. Let your children spoon ingredients into resealable plastic sandwich bags, and then close and shake their bags to mix the ingredients.

Fall

I Like Fall

Sung to: "Skip to My Lou"

Picking apples off the trees,
Jumping in a pile of leaves,
Picking pumpkins from the vine,
I think I like fall just fine.

Diane Thom

Fall Is Here

Sung to: "Three Blind Mice"

Fall is here, fall is here.
Winter's near, winter's near.
See the leaves, red, yellow, and brown,
See the pumpkins on the ground,
See the apples so red and round,
Fall is here.

Gayle Bittinger

Rake the Leaves

Sung to: "The Mulberry Bush"

This is the way we rake the leaves,
Rake the leaves, rake the leaves.
This is the way we rake the leaves,
When fall is here.

Additional verses: This is the way we pick the pumpkins; This is the way we crack the walnuts; This is the way we eat the apples.

Ann-Marie Donovan

Pumpkin Growing

Sung to: "Frère Jacques"

Pumpkin growing, pumpkin growing,
On the ground, on the ground.
How'd you get so big,
How'd you get so big,
Big and round, big and round?

Diane Thom

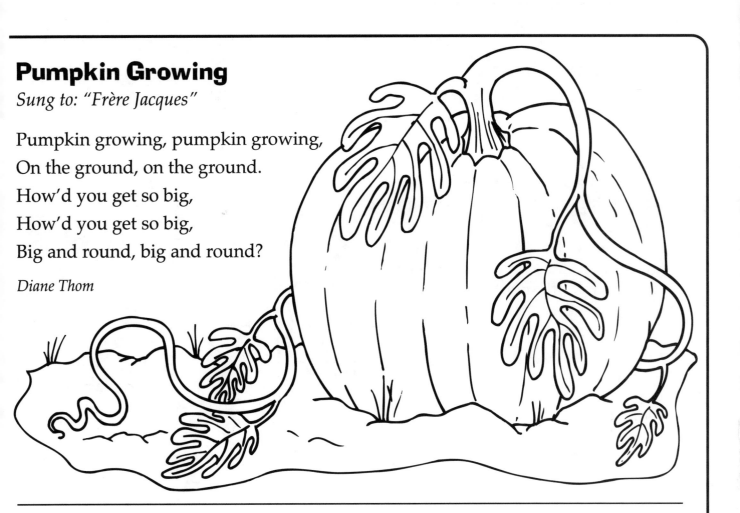

Crunchy Apples

Sung to: "Up on the Housetop"

Crunchy apples, good to eat.
Sometimes tart, and sometimes sweet.
Eat one now, or maybe try
To bake an apple cake or pie.
Ah, ah, ah, so good to eat.
Oh, oh, oh-oh, what a treat!
Shine an apple up and take a bite.
Outside it's red, inside it's white.

Deborah Zumbar

Fall

Fall Nature Walk

Divide your children into small groups. Invite an adult to join each group. Make a copy of the Fall Scavenger Hunt list on page 17 for each group. Talk about the items shown on the list. Have the children think about where they might see each item. Take the children on a nature hike to look for signs of fall. As they see each item on their list, have them check it off. (Perhaps they could keep some of the items to glue on the page. If not, they can draw or cut out pictures.) Encourage the children to look for signs of fall that are not on their list. When you return to your room, let the children talk about what they saw. What animals did they see? What were the animals doing? What was happening to the trees? Were any flowers still blooming?

Fall Picnic

Pack up a picnic with some fall treats such as apple slices, apple cider, and pumpkin bread. Take your picnic outside to eat. Look all around with your children to find a place to sit where you can observe fall activities together. You could sit by a tree that is losing its leaves or find a place to observe a squirrel getting ready for winter. Enjoy your snack while you quietly observe fall all around you.

Fall Scavenger Hunt

☐ red leaf

☐ tree with apples on it

☐ yellow leaf

☐ orange pumpkins on a vine

☐ bird flying south

☐ pile of leaves

☐ squirrel collecting nuts

☐ empty bird nest

☐ tree with no leaves

☐ _____

☐ brown grass

☐ _____

Winter

Snow Painting

When snow is covering the ground, take your children outside for some Snow Painting. Fill spray bottles with water and add a different shade of food coloring to each one. Let the children take turns spraying the snow with the colored water to create designs.

Snow Sculptures

After a big snowfall, invite your children outside to make Snow Sculptures. Let them decide how they would like to work (alone, in pairs, or in teams) to build the snow creations of their choice. Encourage them to think about what they want their sculptures to look like: big or small, long or short, plain or decorated. When everyone is finished, take pictures of them standing beside their completed sculptures. Put the photos in a Snow Sculpture book to enjoy throughout the winter.

Variation: Let your children build Snow Castles instead. Show them how to pack snow in plastic buckets and other containers, turn them upside down on the ground, and lift them up to leave mounds of snow. (Spray the containers with nonstick cooking spray to prevent the snow from sticking.)

Extension: Hand out awards for the finished creations using construction paper and markers. Include awards such as biggest, smallest, funniest, scariest, and snowiest.

Icicle Painting

Using powdered tempera paint, prepare paint slightly thicker than normal. Give each of your children a sheet of construction paper and an icicle (with no sharp edges) or an ice cube. Spoon a small amount of the thickened paint onto each child's paper. Let the children use their icicles to "paint" a picture.

Ice Sculpting

Place a block of ice in a dishpan. Put a small bowl of rock salt and a spoon close by. Let the children take turns spooning the salt on the ice. Wherever the rock salt touches the ice, the ice will melt faster, leaving a pattern of holes. In addition, set out three eyedroppers and three small containers filled with diluted red, yellow, and blue food coloring. Let the children drop the colors on the ice. As the ice melts, the colors will run together and produce secondary colors.

Shadow Art

It's fun to explore shadows when the groundhog peeks its head out to see if spring is around the corner. Take your children outside on a sunny winter day to make Shadow Art. Divide the children into pairs. Give each pair a sheet of construction paper. Let the children in each pair take turns being the artist and the audience: the artist will hold the paper so that the shadow of an object falls on it while the audience tells what he or she likes about the shadow. Have them trade places and repeat. How many different shadow shapes can they make?

Shadow Boards

Provide each of your children with a paper plate or a piece of cardboard and a collection of small objects such as pebbles, nutshells, pasta pieces, buttons, and paper scraps. Let them glue the objects onto their plates. When the plates are dry, have the children take them outside to observe what kind of shadows they make. Encourage the children to hold their plates in a variety of positions to cast different shadow shapes.

Icy Winter

Read the poem below out loud.
See if your children can
discover the fun surprise. (*Icy*
can also be read as *I see*.)

Icy you and icy me,

Icy branches on each tree.

Icy patterns on the glass,

Icy steps we have to pass.

Icy walks and roads galore,

Icy wintertime once more.

Icy vines upon the wall,

Icy scenes I now recall.

Jean Warren

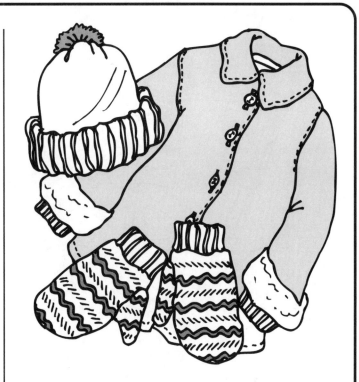

Put on Your Mittens

Have your children act out the
motions as you read the rhyme
below to them.

Put on your mittens,

Put on your hat,

Put on your coat,

Just like that.

Go outside

To play in the snow,

Have some fun,

Then inside you go.

Take off your mittens,

Take off your hat,

Take off your coat,

Just like that.

Gayle Bittinger

Icy Math

Make ice cubes in a variety of sizes and shapes. (Unique ice cube trays can be found in many kitchen stores.) Set out a handful of the ice cubes on a tray or a baking sheet. Encourage your children to count, sort, and make patterns with the ice cubes. Have new ice cubes on hand (in a nearby freezer or a portable cooler, if you wish) to replace ice cubes as they melt.

Snow Cards

Set out five sheets of construction paper. Number the sheets of paper from 1 to 5 by drawing a different number of circles on each paper to make Snow Cards. Cover the cards with clear self-stick paper. If you have snow, let your children take the cards outside and set them on a flat surface. Have them make a snowball to place on each circle. Ask them to count the snowballs on each Snow Card. If there's no snow, give your children white modeling dough to shape into balls and place on the Snow Cards.

Frozen Bubbles

Chill containers of bubble solution in the refrigerator. When the temperature is below freezing, take your children outside to blow bubbles. Have them observe the bubbles closely as they blow. They will notice ice crystals forming on the surface of the bubbles. What happens when the bubbles pop? (They shatter.)

Snow Tracks

Encourage your children to be detectives by looking for tracks in the snow and trying to identify who made the tracks. If they look closely, they may see tracks left by people, dogs, cats, birds, or other animals.

Winter

Winter Movement Fun

Have your children lie on the floor to form a beautiful blanket of "snow." Next, have them pretend that children are rolling them up to make large snowballs until they become so large they have to stand up and become snowmen. Now take them on a winter adventure as you lead them through the activities described below.

Marching and Skating—Tell your children that the snowmen are so excited that they can move that they start marching, skipping, and running all around. Then let them pretend to join some winter skaters at a frozen pond and skate around the room.

Snowmen—Explain to your children that because they are snowmen, they must stand frozen and stiff. Then tell them that one day, the sun shines a little warmer, and they begin to thaw slightly. Call out body parts for the children to start moving. Have them begin moving these parts slowly until their whole bodies are moving.

Melting—Pretend to be the sun and shine down on the snowmen. Tell the children that they get weaker and weaker as it gets hotter and hotter, until they gradually melt away. Encourage the children to melt slowly and gracefully to the floor.

Rice Cake Snow Creatures

Give each of your children three small rice cakes. Let the children spread the rice cakes with whipped cream and decorate them with raisins to make Snow Creatures.

Icicle Pops

Blend together 2 cups plain yogurt, 2 sliced bananas, 2 teaspoons vanilla, and 2 cups fruit juice or fruit chunks. Pour the mixture into small paper cups arranged on a baking sheet. Cover with plastic wrap. If the temperature is below freezing, place the baking sheet outside. (If the temperature is above freezing, place the baking sheet in a freezer.) When the yogurt mixture is half frozen, place a small plastic spoon in each cup. Makes 8 to 10 small Icicle Pops.

Mashed Potato Snowballs

Let your children help you mold mashed potatoes into small snowballs and put them on a baking sheet. Give them grated Monterey jack cheese to sprinkle on top of the snowballs. Bake the snowballs at 400°F until the cheese is melted, about 10 minutes. Cool and eat.

Winter

Sing a Song of Winter
Sung to: "Sing a Song of Sixpence"

Sing a song of winter,
Frost is in the air.
Sing a song of winter,
Snowflakes everywhere.
Sing a song of winter,
Hear the sleigh bells chime.
Can you think of anything
As nice as wintertime?

Let your child name other signs
of winter.

Judith McNitt

The Winter Wind
Sung to: "Happy Birthday"

The winter wind blows.
The winter wind blows.
It gives me the shivers
From my head to my toes!

Marie Cecchini

Ice and Snow
Sung to: "Jingle Bells"

Ice and snow, cold winds blow,
Hop aboard our sleigh.
Oh, what fun it is to play
Winter games today.
Ice and snow, cold winds blow,
Let's be on our way.
Oh, what fun it is to play
Winter games today.

Betty Silkunas

Where's Your Shadow?

Sung to: "Frère Jacques"

Where's your shadow?
Where's your shadow?
Turn around, it's on the ground.
Can you make it jump up?
See if you can catch it.
Run around, run around.

Heather Tekavec

Who Is Made of Snow?

Sung to: "Do Your Ears Hang Low?"

Who is made of snow
When the temperature is low?
Who stands outside
When the ground is cold and white?
Who starts to melt
When the warm sunshine is felt?
Who is made of snow?

Diane Thom

Walking on the Ice

Sung to: "The Farmer in the Dell"

Walking on the ice,
Walking on the ice.
Don't fall down—
You'll hit the ground!
Walking on the ice.

Have your children remove their shoes and
pretend to walk or skate on ice. Encourage
them to think of action words such as
skating or *sliding* to substitute for *walking*.

Colleen Stockton

Winter

Signs of Winter

Take your children on a walk outside in the wintry weather. Encourage them to look for signs that winter has arrived. For example, they could look for changes in the weather (colder, there may be snow or rain), in plants and animals (some trees lose their leaves, most flowers are gone, many animals are hibernating or have gone to warmer climates), or in the clothes people wear. If you wish, copy the Winter Changes list on page 29. Take it along with you on your walk. As your children mention or see changes, write them down in the appropriate sections. When you get back to your room, discuss all the changes they saw.

Sounds of Winter

Go on a winter walk. Listen carefully with your children for winter sounds. Encourage them to think about how they are different from summer sounds. Are things noisier or quieter? What animals can they hear? What people noises do they hear?

Winter Picnic

Pack up some hot chocolate and crackers, and take your children on a picnic to enjoy the winter landscape. Be sure to dress for the weather. Bring blankets to sit on as you enjoy your hot chocolate together and look for all the signs of winter that you can see.

Winter Changes

Changes in the Weather

Changes in Plants and Animals

Changes in Clothing

Other Changes We Saw

Spring

Spring Tree Art

Several days before this activity, let your children begin making paper dots. Provide them with a supply of pink paper. Let them use a hole punch to punch out dots. When you have a fair amount of pink dots, use a crayon to draw a bare tree on a piece of paper for each child. Let your children brush glue over their tree branches and sprinkle on the pink dots.

Window Garden

Cover a table with an old vinyl tablecloth and set out squeeze bottles of colored glue. (Either purchase colored glue or make your own by adding food coloring to white glue.) Invite your children to squirt the glue on the table to make raised flower designs. For best results, use generous amounts of thick glue. Let the flower shapes dry overnight. When the glue is dry, peel the shapes from the tablecloth. Let your children arrange their flowers on the windows of your room to make a festive Window Garden.

Blossoms

Set out sponge dish scrubbers (the kind sold at supermarkets for washing drinking glasses) and paint in pastel colors. On a sheet of butcher paper, draw stems with a green crayon. Let your children press the dish mops into the paint and then onto the paper to print "blossoms" all over the stems.

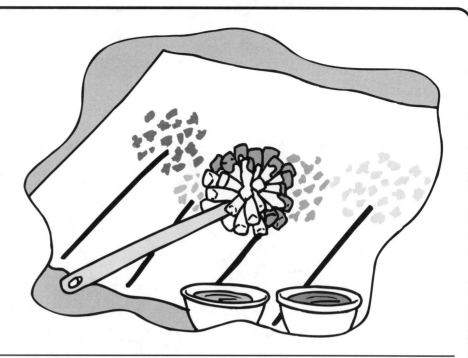

Sidewalk Artistry

A few hours after a spring rainfall, take your children outdoors and let them draw on the wet pavement with sidewalk chalk. The water will turn the chalk hues into brilliant colors.

Mini Windsocks

Let your children decorate cardboard tubes as desired. Cut crepe-paper streamers into narrow strips. Have the children glue several of the strips to one end of their tubes. Then tie a loop of string to the other end of each tube for a hanger.

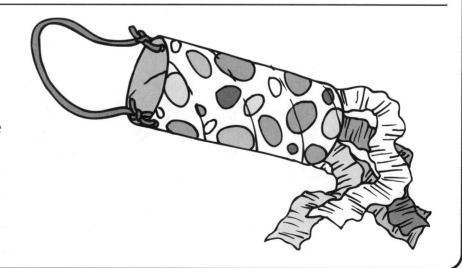

Spring

Chicks

Trace around each child's foot on a piece of yellow construction paper. After cutting out the foot shape, have the child glue it, toes pointing down, on a piece of white or light blue construction paper. Then show the child how to draw an eye, a beak, and legs on the shape to turn it into a "chick," as shown in the illustration.

Little Lambs

Help each of your children make a construction paper hand shape with thumb and fingers outstretched. Turn the shape upside down so that the thumb becomes a lamb's neck and head and the fingers become the legs. Let each child glue stretched-out cotton balls on the lamb's body and a cotton tuft on the lamb's head. Then have the child draw an eye with a crayon or a felt tip marker.

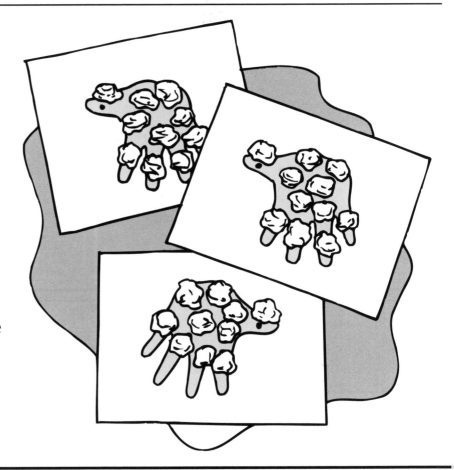

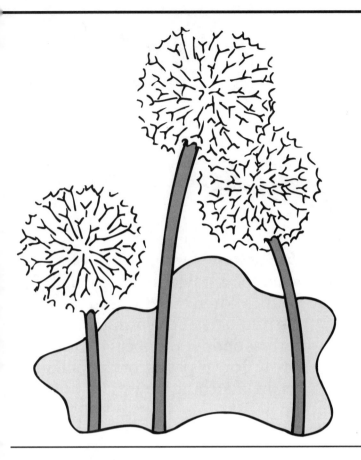

Dandelion Wishes

Take your children outside to hunt for wispy dandelions. Tell them about the tradition of blowing away the dandelion seeds and making a wish. Then let your children make dandelion wishes. Teach them the rhyme below.

I have a dandelion today
Whose golden hair has turned to gray.
And when I blow on it like so,

(Blow dandelion.)

Way up in the air its hair will go!

Lois E. Putnam

Five Umbrellas

Sit under an umbrella and read the poem below out loud to your children.

Five umbrellas stood by the back door,
The red one went outside, then there were four.

Four umbrellas pretty as can be,
The blue one went outside, then there were three.

Three umbrellas with nothing to do,
The green one went outside, then there were two.

Two umbrellas not having much fun,
The yellow one went outside, then there was one.

Just one umbrella alone in the hall,
The purple one went outside, and that was all.

Jean Warren

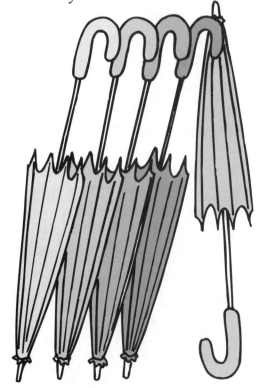

Spring

Natural Counting

Collect flowers, small tree branches, or plants. Set them outside on the grass and let your children take turns guessing how many petals are on the flowers or how many leaves are on the tree branches or plants. Then help the children count the actual number of petals and leaves.

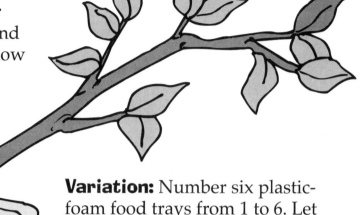

Variation: Number six plastic-foam food trays from 1 to 6. Let your children take turns identifying the numbers and placing the corresponding numbers of blades of grass, flower petals, or dandelions on the matching trays.

The Shape of Nature

Gather bunches of differently-shaped leaves and different kinds of flowers. Have your children look at the leaves and flowers and point out as many shapes as they can see, such as ovals and circles in leaves, and lines and points in flowers.

Sizing Up Nature

Show your children three different trees and ask them which tree is the tallest and which is the shortest. Using the same trees, have your children find the one with the biggest trunk and the one with the smallest trunk. Have your children look up at the sky and pick out the smallest and the largest clouds. Show your children three blades of grass and let them choose the shortest and longest blades.

Sensing Spring

Help your children learn about spring by experiencing it through all of their senses. The activities below give you suggestions for stimulating all of the senses.

Seeing—Expose your children to art. Take a trip to the library and check out books about famous artists. Together, look for paintings of flowers and other signs of spring.

Hearing—Listen to the wind. Hang up a set of wind chimes to hear music every time the wind blows.

Touching—Arrange for some bunnies to visit your group. Gently touch their soft fur. (Contact your local Future Farmers of America chapter or a veterinarian for assistance.)

Smelling—Take your children on a smell walk. Stroll outdoors and follow your noses. What do you notice? Wet grass? Springtime blossoms?

Tasting—Provide tender carrots, new potatoes, and other fresh fruits and vegetables for your children to sample.

Spring

Wind in Our Scarves

Give each of your children a silk or nylon scarf. (A secondhand store is a great place to find these inexpensively, or ask parents and friends for donations of outdated scarves.) Have the children pretend their scarves are the wind. Ask them to show you how the "wind" can be a gentle spring breeze or a wild storm.

Baby Chick Dance

Let your children pretend to be baby chicks as you sing the song below. Encourage them to act out the motions as they are described.

Sung to: "Skip to My Lou"

Come baby chicks, time to move,
Stand on your feet, time to groove.
Move back and forth, swing and sway,
Baby chick dancers move this way.

Cheep, cheep, cheep, scratch your feet,
Cheep, cheep, cheep, to the beat.
Cheep, cheep, cheep, turn around,
Cheep, cheep, cheep, now sit down.

Jean Warren

Cheep, cheep, cheep, scratch your feet, ...

Bunny Biscuits

For each of your children, set out a small square of aluminum foil with two uncooked refrigerator biscuits on it, a plastic knife, and three raisins. Have your children cut one of their biscuits in half. Show them how to arrange the two halves at the top of their other biscuit to make bunny "ears." Let them add two raisin eyes and a raisin nose to complete their bunnies. Use a pencil to write each child's name on his or her piece of foil. Place the Bunny Biscuits with the foil underneath them on baking sheets. Bake the biscuits according to the package directions. Allow the Bunny Biscuits to cool slightly before eating them.

Fresh Green Dip

In a blender, whirl together ½ cup cooked fresh or thawed frozen peas, ¼ cup plain yogurt, and a dash garlic powder (optional) until smooth. Or, let your children take turns mashing the ingredients together with a potato masher. Serve with the children's favorite raw vegetables, including some fresh spring veggies such as asparagus, snap peas, and baby carrots.

Spring

Spring Senses

Sung to: "Frère Jacques"

I see spring, I see spring,
Rainbows bright, rainbows bright.
Red, orange, yellow.
Green, blue, and purple.
I see spring, I see spring.

I hear spring, I hear spring,
Tweet, tweet, tweet; tweet, tweet, tweet.
Pitter-patter raindrops,
Pitter-patter raindrops.
I hear spring, I hear spring.

I touch spring, I touch spring,
Baby chicks, baby chicks.
Soft little bunnies,
Soft little bunnies.
I touch spring, I touch spring.

I smell spring, I smell spring,
Spring blossoms, spring blossoms.
Perfume in the air,
Flowers everywhere.
I smell spring, I smell spring.

I taste spring, I taste spring,
Baby carrots, baby carrots.
Tasty little peas,
Tasty little peas.
I taste spring, I taste spring.

Jean Warren

Birds Are Busy

Sung to: "Mary Had a Little Lamb"

Birds are busy building nests,
Building nests, building nests.
Birds are busy building nests,
Spring is everywhere.

Cynthia Walters

It Is Raining

Sung to: "Frère Jacques"

It is raining,
It is raining.
Drip, drip, drop.
Drip, drip, drop.
See the little raindrops,
Hear them as they plip-plop.
Drip, drip, drop.
Drip, drip, drop.

Gayle Bittinger

In My Flower Garden

Sung to: "Down by the Station"

Out in my garden
Early in the morning,
See the pretty flowers
Standing in a row.
See the rows of daisies
And the rows of sweet peas.
Hoe-hoe, grow-grow,
In my garden, please.

Jean Warren

Spring

Spring Colors

Take your children outside to explore the colors of spring. Photocopy the Spring Colors Graph on page 41 and attach it to a clipboard. Use a crayon to color over each color word in the matching color. Each time your children find something that is one of the colors on the graph, put a check next to that color. When you get back inside, have the children talk about all the colors they saw. Ask them to look at the graph and tell you which color they saw the most and which one they saw the least.

Variation: Divide your children into pairs. Give each pair a clipboard with the Spring Colors Graph attached. Have them put check marks next to the colors they see. When you go inside, make a large group chart and put everyone's results together. Encourage the children to talk about the results.

Spring Picnic

Pack up a simple snack, such as cheese and crackers, and take your children outside for snacktime. Spread several blankets out on the ground where your children will be able to enjoy the sights, scents, and sounds of spring. As you share your snack, talk quietly about what they are observing, smelling, and hearing. How are these sounds different from the ones they hear in other seasons?

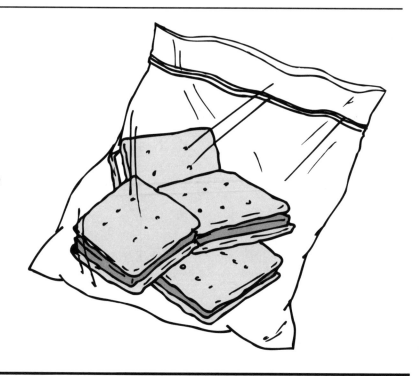

Spring Colors Graph

red	
yellow	
orange	
blue	
green	
purple	

Summer

Sunshine Art

Set out shallow containers of yellow, red, and orange tempera paint. Let your children dip round-shaped objects into the paint to make sun prints on blue construction paper. Have them try using the end of a washed and dried corncob, the head of a daisy or dandelion flower, a wooden spoon, or a plastic drinking glass.

Blue Skies

Have your children use crayons to draw summer scenes on white construction paper. Encourage them to think about all of the things they see in the summer. When they are finished, let them paint blue watercolor all over their drawings to create "blue skies."

Chalk People

One at a time, have your children lie down on a flat, paved surface (such as a driveway or patio) while you trace around them with sidewalk chalk. Have them look at their outlines. Encourage them to add details to their outlines, such as eyes, nose, mouth, ears, and hair. Let them add clothes if they wish. For more interest, let them lie down for another tracing, this time with their arms outstretched or their legs bent as if jumping.

Hmmm, this is squishy.

Sand Dough

Mix together 2 cups all-purpose flour, 1 cup salt, 1 cup water, and a few drops of vegetable oil. Add ½ to ¾ cup sand until the dough is the desired texture. Let your children play with the Sand Dough and encourage them to describe how it feels.

Water Designs

Let your children turn dry patios and fences into temporary pieces of artwork. Give your children spray bottles filled with water. Have them spray the water on the patio or fence and watch the designs the water makes. Ask them to notice how the water quickly evaporates (depending on how hot it is), leaving the patio or fence ready for new Water Designs.

Summer

The Beach

This is a wonderful story to use with your children after a summer trip to the beach. If you can't take a real trip, then take a pretend one with your children, and let them imagine their answers to the beach story below.

I went to the beach today.

The sun was as hot as _____.

The sky was as blue as _____.

The water was as cold as _____.

I swam in the water just like a _____.

I played in the sand and built a _____.

While I was digging in the sand, I found a _____.

I love to run on the beach like a _____.

I had fun at the beach.

Jean Warren

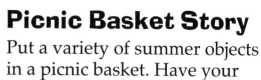

Picnic Basket Story

Put a variety of summer objects in a picnic basket. Have your children sit around the basket. Begin telling them a story about summer. Let the children take turns reaching into the basket and pulling out an object for you to incorporate into your story.

Variation: If your children are older, let them pull the items out of the basket and continue the story themselves.

Shell Game

Hide an object under one of three shells lined up in a row. Then move the shells around and have your children guess which shell the object is hidden under. Let them take turns hiding the object for each other, too.

Hint: Shells can often be purchased inexpensively at import stores or craft shops. Or, check with local fish markets to see if they will let you have discarded shells or shell pieces.

Shell Hunt

Fill a pail or a dishpan half full with sand. Mix in some small shells. Invite one of your children to dig for shells. When the child is finished, help him or her count the shells. Then have the child place the shells on a piece of paper and draw a circle around each one. Write the corresponding numeral at the top of the page. Repeat with each child.

Shell Match-Ups

Collect pairs of different kinds of shells. Set out the shells in a random order. Let your children take turns finding the shells that match.

Shell Counting Game

With a felt tip marker, divide a paper plate into four to eight wedges (depending on your children's abilities). Number the wedges, starting with 1. Give each of your children a numbered plate and some small shells. Have the children identify each numeral and count out the corresponding number of shells to place on each wedge.

Summer

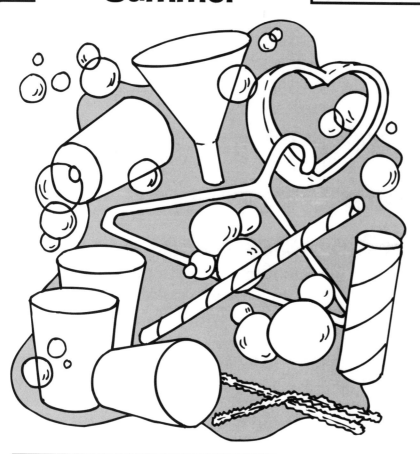

Bubble Blowers

Challenge your children to use various objects to create unique bubble blowers. Place several shallow pans outside and fill them with bubble solution. To get your children thinking, set out several of these items for them to use as they create their own bubble blowers: paper cups, straws, pipe cleaners, soft-drink holders, funnels, cookie cutters, toilet tissue tubes, and plastic hangers.

Bubble Experiments

As your children blow their bubbles, have them notice that not all bubbles behave the same way. As they experiment, ask the following questions: What happens if you blow hard? If you blow softly? What color are the bubbles? Are all the bubbles the same shape? The same size? What happens when you touch a bubble? How long do bubbles last?

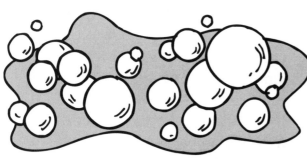

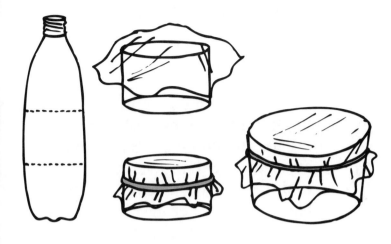

Underwater Viewer

Cut a section out of the middle of a plastic soft-drink bottle as shown in the illustration. Cover one end of the bottle with plastic wrap. Secure the wrap with a large rubber band. Press the covered end into a tub of water filled with sand, shells, small toys, etc. Let the children look through it to see below the surface of the water.

Water Magnifier

To make the magnifier, you will need a plastic container with lid (margarine and whipped topping containers work well), plastic wrap, a penny, and water. Remove the lid from the container and use a craft knife to cut out the center of the lid. Cut the bottom off of the container. Spread a piece of plastic wrap over the rim of the container. Place a penny in the center of the wrap to weigh it down a bit and then place the lid on top. Next, pour water over the top, filling the plastic wrap. Remove the penny. (The water turns the plastic wrap into a concave lens. Objects viewed through this lens will appear magnified.)

To use the viewer, place a small object, like a button, under the container and another alongside it. Let your children notice how the button viewed through the water looks larger. Let your children choose other objects to view through the lens. Children will find it easier to notice the enlargement if they can compare the magnified object to an identical object outside the viewer.

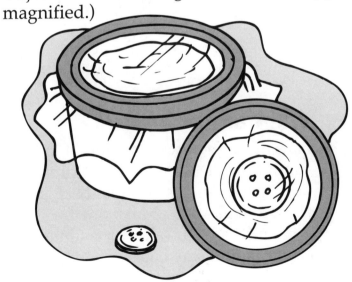

Summer

Bare Feet Wiggles

First, have your children remove their shoes and socks. Ask them to sit on the floor and concentrate on their feet, rubbing them against each other, wiggling their toes, knocking their big toes together, bobbing their heels, and bending their legs and stamping their feet. Now, have them stand up. Have them pretend they are walking on a warm sunny beach in their bare feet. How does the sand feel? How would they walk barefooted over snow, some rocks, a log with slivers, grass, mud, soft carpet?

Summer Games

Many special athletic events happen over the summer. Have your own backyard games. Try games such as Balance on the Beam (on a two-by-four), Jump Over the Pillows, and the Flying Disk Throw. Make medals by covering cardboard circles with foil. Give one to each child who participates.

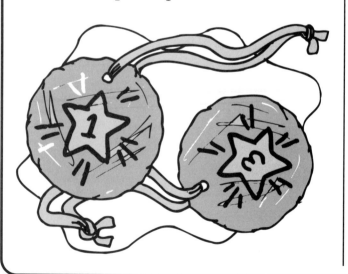

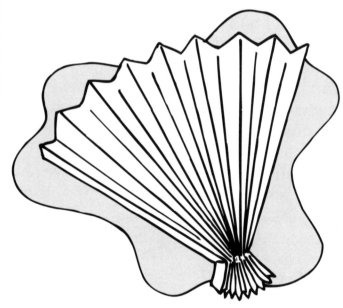

The Fan Club

Fans are a great way to cool off in the summer heat. Show your children how to fold sheets of paper back and forth to make fans. Make one for yourself, as well. Take turns fanning each other to stay cool.

Red, White, and Blueberry Parfaits

Set out bowls of sliced strawberries, vanilla yogurt, and blueberries. Give each of your children a clear-plastic cup. Help your children place a scoop of red strawberries, a scoop of white yogurt, and a scoop of blue blueberries into their cups. Enjoy!

Watermelon Juice

Cut a seedless watermelon into small chunks. Put several chunks in a resealable plastic bag for each child. Refrigerate the bags until they are needed. Give each child one of the watermelon bags. Show your children how to gently squeeze their bags, squishing the watermelon to make "juice." When their Watermelon Juice is ready, give them straws they can use to drink it through an opening in the seal.

Frosty Fruit

Let your children help you spread sliced fruit on a foil-covered baking sheet. Freeze for 3 hours, then eat. Try some of the following fruits: banana, cantaloupe, seedless grapes (red seedless are especially tasty), and watermelon.

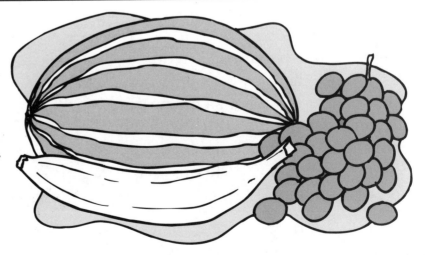

Summer

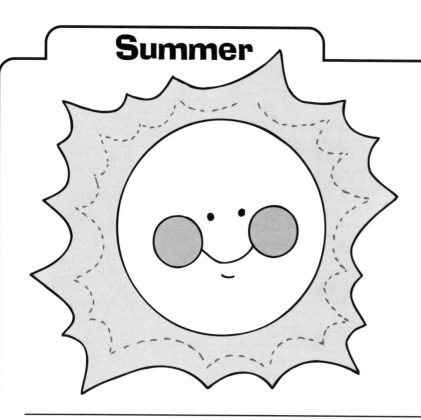

Summertime

Sung to: "Jingle Bells"

Summertime, summertime,
Summertime is here.
Warm, hot sun, and water fun,
Best time of the year!
Summertime, summertime,
Summertime is here.
Oh, what fun is summertime,
My favorite time of year!

Kathleen Soman

Summer Is Such Fun

Sung to: "Old MacDonald Had a Farm"

Summer, summer is such fun,
Yes, oh, yes, it is.
There's so much that you can do,
Yes, oh, yes, there is.
You can go to the pool and keep real cool,
Jump right in and take a swim,
Pretend to be a fish with fins.
Summer, summer is such fun,
Yes, oh, yes, it is.

Summer, summer is such fun,
Yes, oh, yes, it is.
There's so much that you can do,
Yes, oh, yes, there is.
You can hear a band or sit on the sand,
Play in the sea or play catch with me,
Run and hide from a bumblebee.
Summer, summer is such fun,
Yes, oh, yes, it is.

Barbara B. Fleisher

Summer's Here!

Sung to: "Frère Jacques"

Days are longer,
Sunshine's stronger.
Summer's here! Summer's here!
Let's jump through the sprinkler,
Let's make lemonade,
Summer's here! Summer's here!

Diane Thom

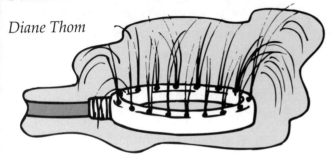

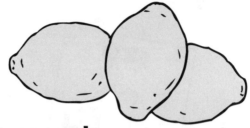

Lemonade

Sung to: "I'm a Little Teapot"

On a sunny day, my daddy made
Frosty, cold lemonade.
Juicy lemons, sugar,
Water, and ice.
Making lemonade is nice!

Ruth Cox Anderson

Summer Treat

Sung to: "Teddy Bear, Teddy Bear"

Ice cream cone, ice cream cone,
Cold and sweet.

   (Shiver.)

Ice cream cone, ice cream cone,
Summer treat.

   (Raise hands above head to represent sun.)

Ice cream cone, ice cream cone,
Melts so quick.

   (Bend legs and lower self to ground.)

Ice cream cone, ice cream cone,
Lick, lick, lick!

   (Lick lips.)

Diane Thom

Summer

Summer Walk

Make a copy the Signs of Summer list on page 53. Plan a walk with your children to search for signs of summer. Before you leave, go over the Signs of Summer list with your children. Let them think of other things to add to the list. Take the list with you when you go on your walk. Put a check mark by each of the signs your children find. For more fun, give each child a copy of the page. They can draw or cut out pictures of these summer signs.

Summer Picnic

Let your children help you pack a picnic snack. Be sure to pack a few special summer fruits, such as watermelon slices and grapes. Spread a blanket outdoors in the shade of a tree. Enjoy your picnic together. When you are finished, lie back on the blanket and watch the clouds and birds float by.

Signs of Summer

☐ sun

☐ people wearing sandals

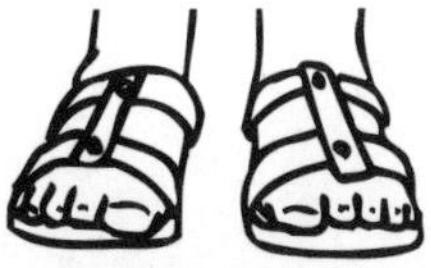

☐ flowers

☐ fruit on bushes or trees

☐ gardens

☐ car with open window

☐ blue skies

☐ wading pool

☐ sprinklers

☐ _____

☐ people wearing shorts

☐ _____

Animals

Forest

Fuzzy Bears

Cut a bear shape for each child out of brown construction paper or posterboard. (Use the pattern on page 67.) Let your children brush glue all over their shapes. Then have them sprinkle sawdust on top of the glue to represent fur.

Fishing Game

Cut fish shapes (see pattern on page 67) for each of your children out of red, yellow, and blue construction paper. Make a "river" by arranging two long pieces of blue yarn on the floor about a foot apart. Place the fish in the river and have the children pretend to be bears. Ask each child in turn to catch a red fish, a yellow fish, etc. Let the "bears" keep the fish that they catch, making sure that everyone ends up with the same number of fish.

Variation: Write different numerals on the fish shapes to make a number recognition game.

Brown Bear, Brown Bear

Read the rhyme below to your children. Have them pretend to be brown bears and act out the motions.

Brown bear, brown bear
Turn around.
Brown bear, brown bear
Touch the ground.
Brown bear, brown bear
Find some honey.
Brown bear, brown bear
Sleep 'til it's sunny.

Adapted Traditional

The Bears Are Walking

Sung to: "When Johnny Comes Marching Home"

The bears are walking through
   the woods
Today, today.
The bears are walking through
   the woods
To eat and play.
They catch some fish and eat them, too.
They munch on berries, quite a few.
Then they run around and
   climb a tree or two.

Jean Warren

Forest

Observing Birds

Prepare Suet Bags (see recipe below) with your children and let them hang the bags on nearby trees. Encourage the children to keep a watch for birds that come to eat from the Suet Bags. What kinds of birds do they see? Ask them to describe the birds that visit the feeders. What color are their feathers? Are they big or small? What sounds do they make?

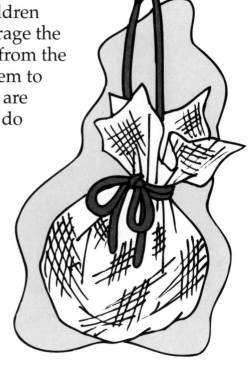

Suet Bags

Cut 6-inch squares out of nylon netting. Mix together suet (available from a butcher) and birdseed. Place a spoonful in the center nylon-netting square. To complete each bag, bring the corners together and tie them with strings.

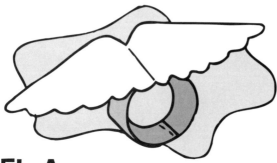

Fly Away

Let your children pretend to be birds. If you wish, make a set of wings for each child by cutting a pair of wing shapes out of construction paper and taping them to his or her wrists. Let your "birds" experiment with their wings. Have them show you how they fly fast and slow, high and low. Ask them to swirl and twirl in the sky as they fly carefully around the room.

Watch the Birds

Sing the song below with your children, letting them pretend to be birds and acting out the motions. Continue with verses about other things birds do such as eat seeds, make nests, and feed their babies.

Sung to: "London Bridge"

Watch the birds as they fly by,
They fly by, they fly by.
Watch the birds as they fly by,
Watch the birds.

Gayle Bittinger

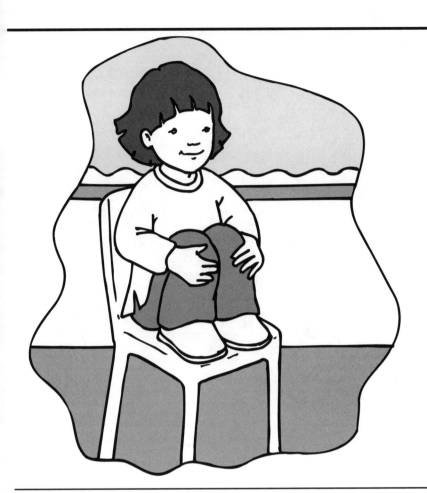

Looks Like an Owl

Have your children sit in a circle and pretend to be owls. Explain to them that owls stay very still and often only move their eyes and heads. Ask them to look at various objects around the room, moving only their eyes or their heads to do so. Then, one at a time, ask each "owl" to fly around the room and find a pretend tree to perch on.

Wise Old Owl

Sung to: "Frère Jacques"

Wise old owl, wise old owl,
In the tree, in the tree.
Whoo-oo are you winking at?
Whoo-oo are you winking at?
Is it me? Is it me?

Jean Warren

Forest

Deer Tracks

Discuss with your children the kinds of tracks different animals make. Show them pictures of deer tracks and other animals' tracks. Talk about how the tracks are made in the snow or dirt. Then let them make their own Deer Tracks. Give the children stamps with deer track shapes, ink pads, and paper. (To make deer track stamps, cut sponge pieces into deer track shapes and glue them to small pieces of wood, as shown in the illustration.) Let the children print deer tracks by pressing the stamps on the ink pads and then on their papers.

Antler Matching

Cut a deer shape with antlers out of several different colors of construction paper. (See pattern on page 68.) Cover the shapes with clear self-stick paper for durability, if desired. Cut the antlers off the deer shapes and place them in a separate pile. Let your children take turns lining up the deer shapes and placing the matching-colored antlers above each deer head.

Flashlight Freeze

Let your children pretend to be deer and have them prance in place. Shine a flashlight on and off. Whenever the "deer" see the light, have them raise their heads high and freeze. When the light goes out, have them start prancing again. Continue the game as long as interest lasts.

Little Deer

Sung to: "Down by the Station"

Down in the woods
Early in the morning,
See the little deer
Looking for some food.
First they eat some leaves,
Then they eat some berries.
Munch, munch, crunch, crunch,
Off they go!

Jean Warren

Forest

Raccoon Touch

Explain to your children that raccoons use their front paws like little hands to search and dig for food. They also appear to enjoy touching and playing with small objects. Let your children pretend to be raccoons and try to identify objects by touch only. In a box, place five or six familiar objects, such as a toy car, a crayon, a plastic egg, a soft sponge, an old toothbrush, and a baby shoe. Have your "raccoons" take turns reaching into the box, grasping an object in their hands, and trying to identify by touch only. When the game is over, let your children find other objects around the room to place in the box. Then start the game again.

Seeing Stripes

Photocopy the raccoon pattern on page 69. Give each of your children a pattern. Have the children notice the stripes on the raccoon's tail. Have the children look around the room or outside to find stripes on other objects. Encourage them to be creative. For example, besides stripes on clothing or a flag, they might see stripes formed by chair slats, window blinds, ladder rungs, ridges in corrugated cardboard, or lines on writing paper. Let each child tell you about the stripes he or she found. Write it on the raccoon pattern.

Forest Snack

Set out bowls of dried fruit and nuts. Explain to your children that raccoons like to eat a variety of foods, including foods like these—fruits and nuts. Have your children pretend to be raccoons as they crawl to the snack table, sit down, and enjoy their special snack.

Raccoon, Raccoon

Sung to: "Twinkle, Twinkle, Little Star"

Raccoon, raccoon, climbing a tree,
Wearing a mask, you can't fool me.
Hiding there so I can't see
What you're doing in that tree.
Raccoon, raccoon, climbing a tree.
Raccoon, raccoon, you can't fool me.

Bonnie Woodard

Forest

Leaping Squirrels

Explain to your children that a tree squirrel uses its thick, plumed tail to help itself balance as it leaps from branch to branch. Stick masking tape "branches" all over your floor. Let your children leap from one branch to another using their "tails" to balance them.

Collecting Nuts

Make five copies of the squirrel pattern on page 69. Number the squirrels from 1 to 5 with numerals and dots. Cut 15 nut shapes from brown construction paper. Let your children take turns placing the correct number of nut shapes on each squirrel.

Pine Cone Hunt

Collect pine cones and hide them around the room where they can be found easily. Let your children pretend to be squirrels. Explain that squirrels gather bushels of pine cones during the fall and store them for the winter. They shred the cones to make bedding and eat the pine nuts that are found in the pine cones. Have your "squirrels" search for the cones while singing the song below. Each time they find a pine cone, have them put it into a box that you have set out to represent a storage place. When all the pine cones have been found, count them together with the children.

Sung to: "Ten Little Indians"

Little gray squirrels looking for pine cones,
Little gray squirrels looking for pine cones,
Little gray squirrels looking for pine cones,
Storing them away for winter.

Jean Warren

I Saw a Little Squirrel

Sung to: "Did You Ever See a Lassie?"

I saw a little squirrel
A-pickin' up acorns.
I saw a little squirrel,
She ran up a tree.
She ran up and ran down
And ran up and ran down.
A busy little squirrel,
As busy as could be.

Becky Valenick

Forest

Animal Riddles

Make up riddles about forest animals. Let your children try to guess which animal you are talking about. For example, you could say this for a deer riddle, "I have four legs. I can run fast. I like to eat leaves and berries. I have antlers. What am I?" Repeat for other forest animals your children know.

I have four legs.
I can run fast.
I like to eat leaves
and berries.

Sorting Animals

Make several copies of each of the animal patterns on pages 67–69. Cut out the animal shapes, and, if desired, color them. Put all the animal shapes together in the pile. Let your children take turns sorting them by kind.

Who Lives in My Tree?

Ask your children to tell you about the many forest animals that live in trees. Then sing the song below with your children, substituting the names of those other animals for *squirrel.*

Sung to: "The Muffin Man"

Do you know who lives in my tree,
Lives in my tree, lives in my tree?
Do you know who lives in my tree?
It is a little squirrel.

Jean Warren

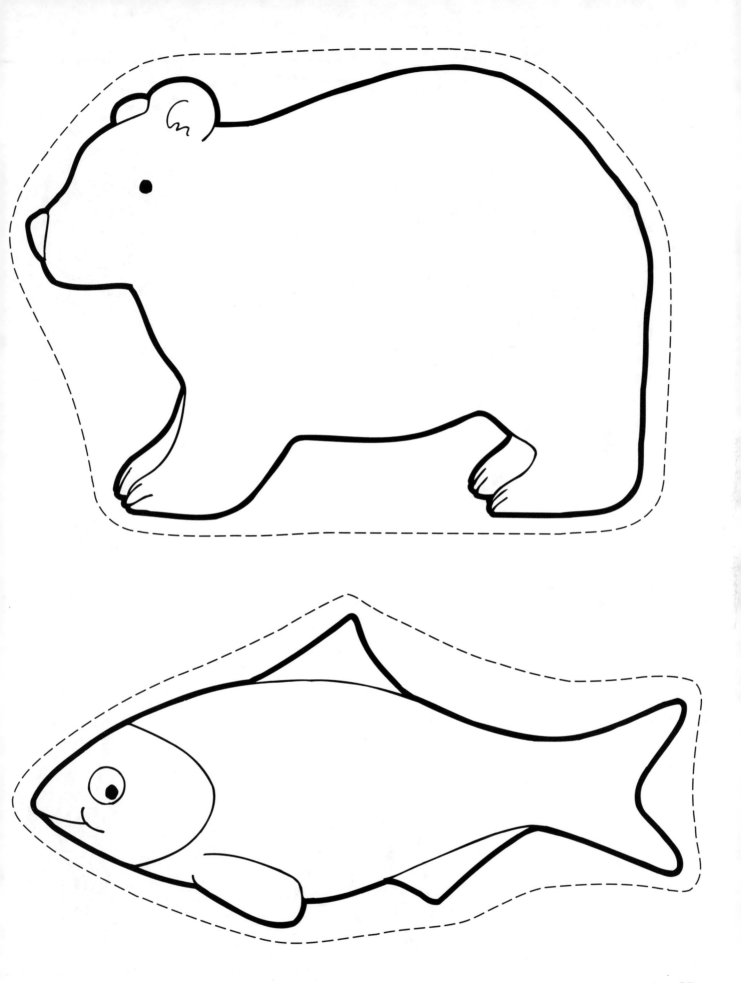

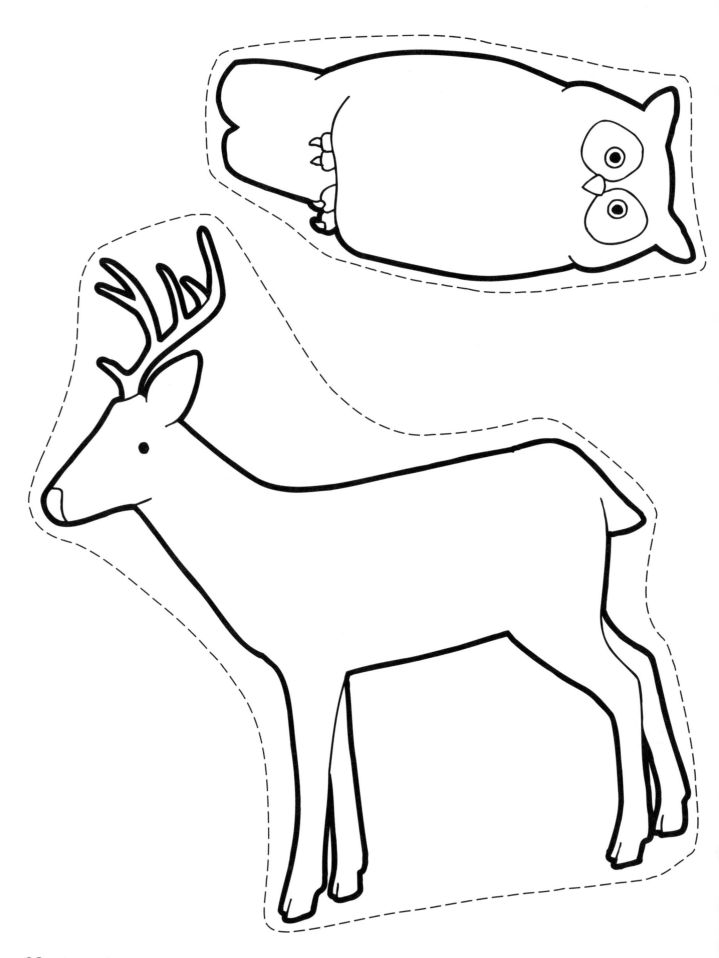

Ocean

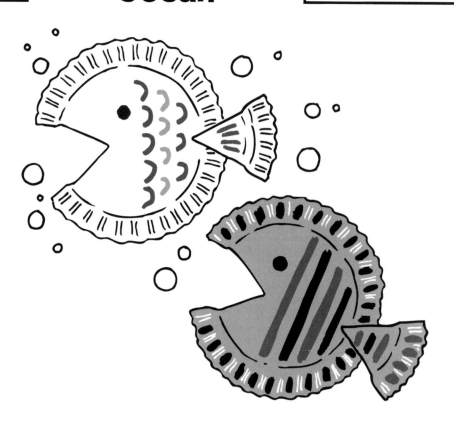

Paper Plate Fish

Give each of your children a paper plate. Show the children how to cut a triangle shape out of one side of a paper plate. Then let each child do this. Have the children glue their triangles to their plates to make tail fins. Let them decorate their fish plates with markers.

Gone Fishing

Cut various sizes of fish shapes out of construction paper. (Use the pattern on page 81 as a guide, if you wish, reducing and enlarging it on a photocopier.) Place the fish shapes in a fish bowl or other container. Set out the fish bowl and a measuring stick a bit longer than half of the fish shapes. Let your children dump the fish shapes out of the bowl and measure them with the measuring stick. If a fish shape is smaller than the measuring stick, have the children put it back in the bowl. If the shape is longer than the stick, let them keep it and say, "It's a keeper."

Extension: Have your children arrange the fish according to size or sort them according to color.

Five Little Fish

Ask your children to stand in place and pretend to be fish. As you say the rhyme below out loud, "catch" one of your fish at the end of each verse and have that child sit down. Repeat the rhyme until all of your fish have been "caught."

Five little fish swimming by the shore.
One got caught, and then there were four.

Four little fish swimming in the sea.
One got caught, and then there were three.

Three little fish swimming in the blue.
One got caught, and then there were two.

Two little fish swimming in the sun.
One got caught, and then there was one.

One little fish swimming for home.
Decided it was best never to roam.

Jean Warren

Swim, Swim

Have your children pretend to be fish. Encourage them to act out the motions as you sing the song below.

Sung to: "Skip to My Lou"

Fish, fish, swim up high,

Fish, fish, swim down low,

Fish, fish, swim so fast,

Fish, fish, swim so slow.

Betty Silkunas

Swimming Octopuses

Cut plain white paper plates in half and cut crepe paper into 12-inch strips. Have your children each select a paper plate half and place it in front of them with the cut side toward them. Give each child two self-stick dots to put on his or her plate for eyes. Let each child then choose eight crepe paper strips and glue them across the bottom of his or her paper plate. Hang the finished octopuses from a string stretched across a window and watch them "swim" as air moves through the room.

Octopus Suction Cups

An octopus has eight arms, or tentacles. On the underside of each tentacle are two rows of small round muscles that act like suction cups. Show your children pictures of an octopus and its tentacles and suckers. Talk about how the octopus uses the suckers to fasten its tentacles tightly to rocks and other objects. Then give each child three or four suction cups in a row cut from an old vinyl bathmat. Let the children try sticking their suction cups to various objects in the room. What things do their cups stick to best?

Hint: The suction cups may stick better if they are moistened first.

Octopus Matching Game

Sometimes an octopus will change its skin color to blend in with its surroundings. Using the pattern on page 81, cut eight octopus shapes out of different colors of felt. Cut simple rock shapes out of the same colors of felt. Place the rock shapes on a flannelboard. Let your children place each octopus shape on the matching rock.

Once I Saw

Sung to: "Did You Ever See a Lassie?"

Once I saw an octopus, octopus, octopus,

Once I saw an octopus down deep in the sea.

Then out came its eight arms,

Its eight arms, its eight arms.

Then out came its eight arms to swim with me!

Sue Schliecker

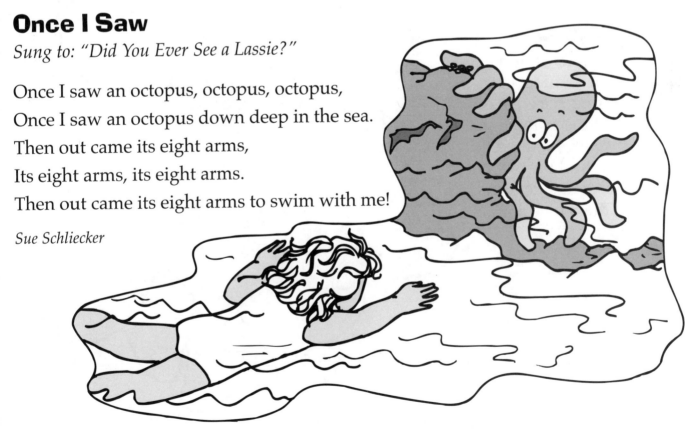

Ocean

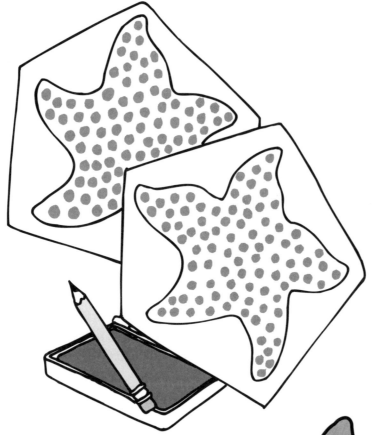

Sea Stars

Draw a sea star shape on a piece of white construction paper. (Use the patterns on page 82 as a guide.) Set out new, unsharpened pencils and red, orange, and purple washable ink pads. Have your children press the pencil erasers on the ink pads and use them like rubber stamps to fill in their sea star shapes with colored dots. Help your children cut out their decorated shapes and glue them on pieces of colored construction paper.

Sea Star Colors

Using the patterns on page 82 as a guide, cut three or four sea stars out of each of the following colors: yellow, orange, pink, red, and purple. Let your children take turns sorting them by color.

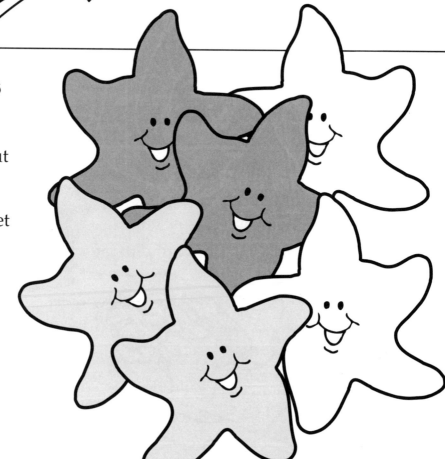

Counting Five

Since most sea stars have five arms, let your children practice counting to five in many different ways. Use the ideas below for counting, or make up your own activities.

* Put away five toys.

* Jump up and down five times.

* Sing five songs.

* Eat five crackers for a snack.

* Make five modeling dough "pancakes."

* Draw five circles.

* Count five pennies.

* Make five wishes.

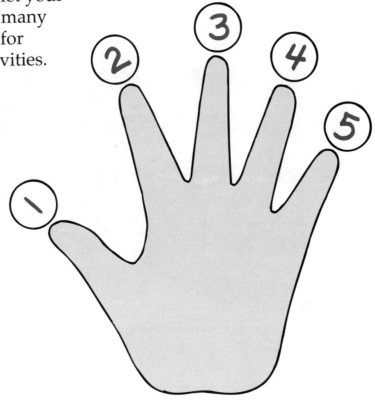

I Am a Sea Star

Sung to: "Up on the Housetop"

I am a sea star, not a fish,
I'll tell you the difference, if you wish.
Fish have fins and swim in schools,
I have feet to wade in tide pools.
Oh, oh, oh, sea star's the name,
Ask me again and I'll tell you the same.
Fish can swim and splash all day,
Stuck to a rock I'd rather stay.

John M. Bittinger

Ocean

Shark Teeth Art

Give each of your children an oval cut out of gray construction paper. Set out black markers, glue, and tooth shapes cut from white construction paper. Let your children glue the tooth shapes on their ovals as shown in the illustration. Then have them add eyes with the markers.

Variation: Let older children cut out their own shark teeth. Give them triangles cut out of white construction paper. Have them cut off the points of the triangles into small "tooth" shapes.

Hunting Game

Explain to your children that a shark has excellent senses of hearing and sight. Then let them practice using their hearing and sight with this game. Set a timer that ticks, and hide it somewhere in your room while the children are not looking. Then have the children use their senses of hearing and sight to find the timer before it goes off. Hide more than one timer, if desired.

Shark Dance

Cut shark fin shapes out of gray construction paper. Attach them to long strips of white construction paper to make "fin" headbands. Fit each of your children with a headband and tape it securely in place. Play some music while your children pretend to be sharks, swimming around the room with their fins showing above the "water."

The Shark

Sung to: "She'll Be Comin' Round the Mountain"

Oh, the shark has lots and lots of big
    sharp teeth,
Oh, the shark has lots and lots of big
    sharp teeth.
Oh, the shark has lots of teeth,
Yes, the shark has lots of teeth.
Oh, the shark has lots and lots of big
    sharp teeth.

Additional verses: Oh, the shark has cartilage for its bones; Oh, the shark can see objects far away.

Susan A. Miller

Beluga Whale Art

For each of your children, prepare a sheet of white construction paper by coloring in several simple beluga whale shapes with a white crayon (be sure to press hard). Prepare a blue paint wash by mixing water into blue tempera paint. Show your children how to make beluga whales appear by painting over their papers with the blue paint wash.

Tail Game

Have your children hold their arms out in front of them and pretend that their arms are whales' tails. Ask them to move their "flukes" up and down. Let them imagine they are swimming through the water. Have them show you how their arms would move if they were swimming quickly. How would they move if they were swimming slowly? What if they were sleeping? Swimming in circles? Let your children "swim" all over the room with their tails pumping up and down.

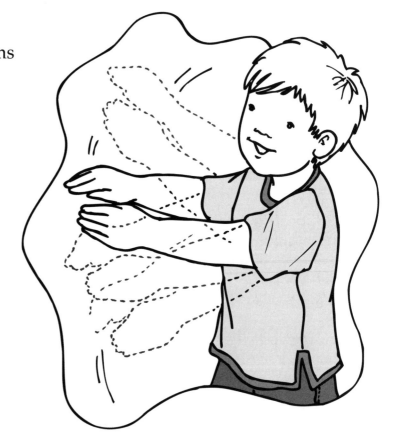

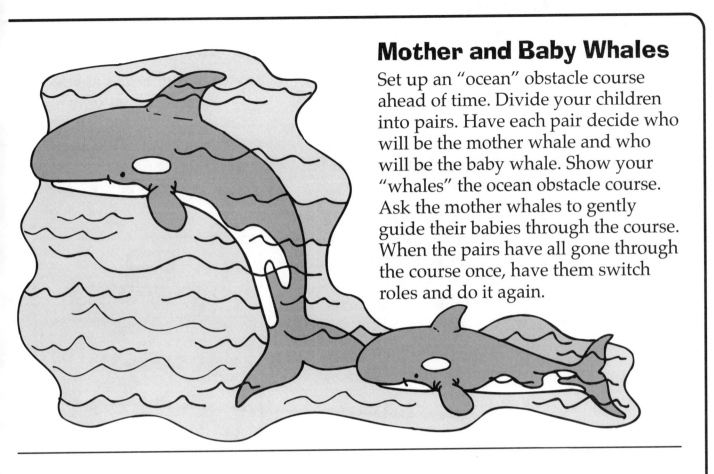

Mother and Baby Whales

Set up an "ocean" obstacle course ahead of time. Divide your children into pairs. Have each pair decide who will be the mother whale and who will be the baby whale. Show your "whales" the ocean obstacle course. Ask the mother whales to gently guide their babies through the course. When the pairs have all gone through the course once, have them switch roles and do it again.

The Whales

Sung to: "I'm a Little Teapot"

See the whales leap and splash,
Leap and splash, leap and splash.
See the whales leap and splash
As on their way they dash.

Hear the whales sing a song,
Sing a song, sing a song.
Hear the whales sing a song
As they swim along.

Gayle Bittinger

Ocean

Ocean Flannelboard

Using the patterns on pages 81–83 as guides, cut the following shapes out of various colors of felt: five fish, four sea stars, three octopuses, two sharks, and one whale. Cut a large boat shape out of brown felt. Cut a blue piece of felt into two large wave shapes.

Place the wave shapes along the bottom of a flannelboard. Place the boat shape on top of the waves. (See illustration.) Place all of the sea life shapes on the waves. As you read the verses below out loud, let your children take turns counting and putting the corresponding shapes in the boat.

Five little fish who lived in the sea,
Jumped in the boat with skipper and me.

Four little sea stars who lived in the sea,
Jumped in the boat with skipper and me.

Three little octopuses who lived in the sea,
Jumped in the boat with skipper and me.

Two little sharks who lived in the sea,
Jumped in the boat with skipper and me.

One little whale who lived in the sea,
Jumped in the boat with skipper and me.

Jean Warren

Variation: Select any five ocean animal patterns to use for this poem. Substitute their names for the ones in the rhyme.

Ocean Corner

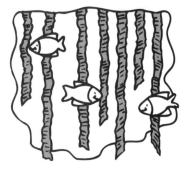

Turn a corner of your room into an ocean playground. Hang green crepe-paper streamers from the ceiling for algae. Place pillow "rocks" all around. Play a tape of ocean wave sounds. Set out books about the ocean. Hang up pictures of ocean plants and animals on the walls. Let your children read and relax in your ocean corner.

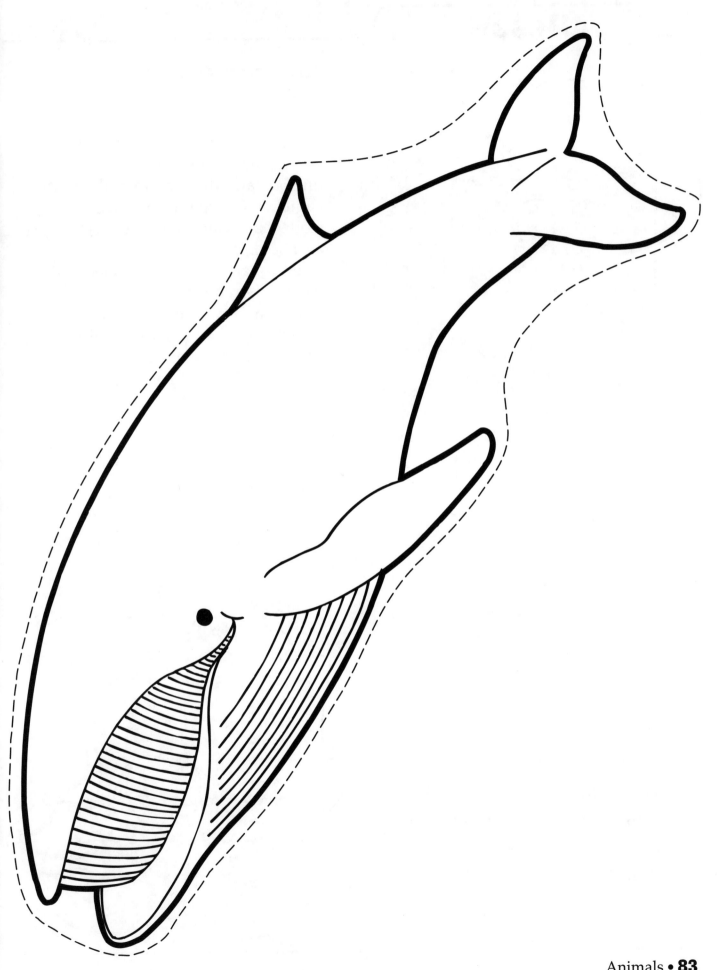

Desert

One and Two

Photocopy the camel patterns on pages 91 and 92 and cut them out. Set out two boxes. Put the picture of the dromedary camel with one hump on one box and the picture of the Bactrian camel with two humps on another box. Collect a variety of single objects such as a book, a comb, a toy car, and a ball. Then collect a variety of object pairs such as two pencils, two shoes, two blocks, and two cups. Mix all the objects together. Let your children take turns sorting the objects into the boxes according to whether there is one or two of the same item.

Camel Song

Sung to: "Old MacDonald Had a Farm"

Here's an animal you should know,
C-A-M-E-L.
For carrying baggage, it's just swell,
C-A-M-E-L.
It's got two humps, or maybe one,
It lives in the desert in the hot, hot sun,
Riding a camel looks like lots of fun.
Here's an animal you should know,
C-A-M-E-L.

Debra Lindahl

Lizard Moves

Talk about the different ways that various kinds of lizards move, such as swimming, sailing from tree to tree, scampering, using their claws to walk upside down on trees and ceilings, crawling on the ground with no legs, and raising their front legs and running. Have your children pretend to be lizards and move in any of those ways.

The Lizards Are Crawling

Sing the song below while your children are moving around like lizards. Substitute the names of other lizard movements such as *sailing, running,* or *scampering* for *crawling.*

Sung to: "When Johnny Comes Marching Home"

The lizards are crawling everywhere,
Hurrah, hurrah.
The lizards are crawling everywhere,
Hurrah, hurrah.
They're crawling 'cross the desert floor,
They're crawling now, and they'll crawl
    some more.
Oh, the lizards, they are crawling everywhere.

Gayle Bittinger

Desert

Ostrich Kicks

Explain to your children that ostriches kick at predators with their strong legs. Take the children to a large open area. Have them pretend to be ostriches. Encourage them to run around and carefully kick with their powerful legs.

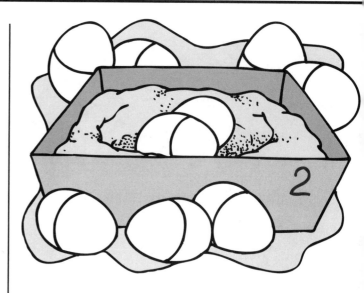

Eggs in Nests

Fill five shoeboxes with sand. Number the boxes from 1 to 5. Dig a shallow "ostrich nest" in each box. Set out the boxes and 15 plastic eggs. Let your children place the appropriate number of eggs in each nest.

Funny Looking Birds

Sung to: "She'll Be Comin' Round the Mountain"

Oh, ostriches are funny looking birds,

Oh, ostriches are funny looking birds.

They can't fly up in the sky,

But they run so quickly by.

Oh, ostriches are funny looking birds.

Pat Beck

Roadrunner Nests

Use the roadrunner pattern on page 93 as a guide for cutting roadrunner shapes out of brown construction paper. Cut small egg shapes out of white construction paper. Set out the roadrunners, eggs, pieces of heavy paper, twigs, and glue. Let your children glue the twigs on their papers in the shape of a nest. Encourage them to pretend that they are roadrunners making their nests. Then have each child glue one of the roadrunner shapes and two to nine egg shapes above his or her completed nest.

When I Race By You

Sung to: "Twinkle, Twinkle, Little Star"

When I race by, oh, so fast,
You will wonder what went past.
I can fly, but I like to run,
All day long in the desert sun.
I use sticks to make my nest,
But I hardly ever rest.

Gayle Bittinger

Snake Designs

Let each of your children decorate a plain white paper plate. Cut the plates into spirals, as shown in the illustration, to make "snakes." Attach a paper clip to each snake shape. Let your children hold onto their snakes to make them dance and slither along on the ground.

Hunting for Vibrations

Have your children put their hands on a table. Hit the table several times with your hand. Explain to your children that what they feel are vibrations. Explain that snakes cannot hear sounds carried in the air as humans do. Instead, they sense vibrations like these on the ground. Have your children hunt around the room for vibrations. (Loud music can make a table vibrate; a refrigerator vibrates when the motor is running; stomping can make the floor vibrate.) Can they make their own vibrations?

Patterned Snakes

Cut 2-by-3-inch sections out of various colors of felt. Cut two snake head shapes and two snake tail shapes out of felt. Place the shapes by a flannelboard. Let your children take turns arranging the heads, sections, and tails on the flannelboard to make brightly patterned snakes.

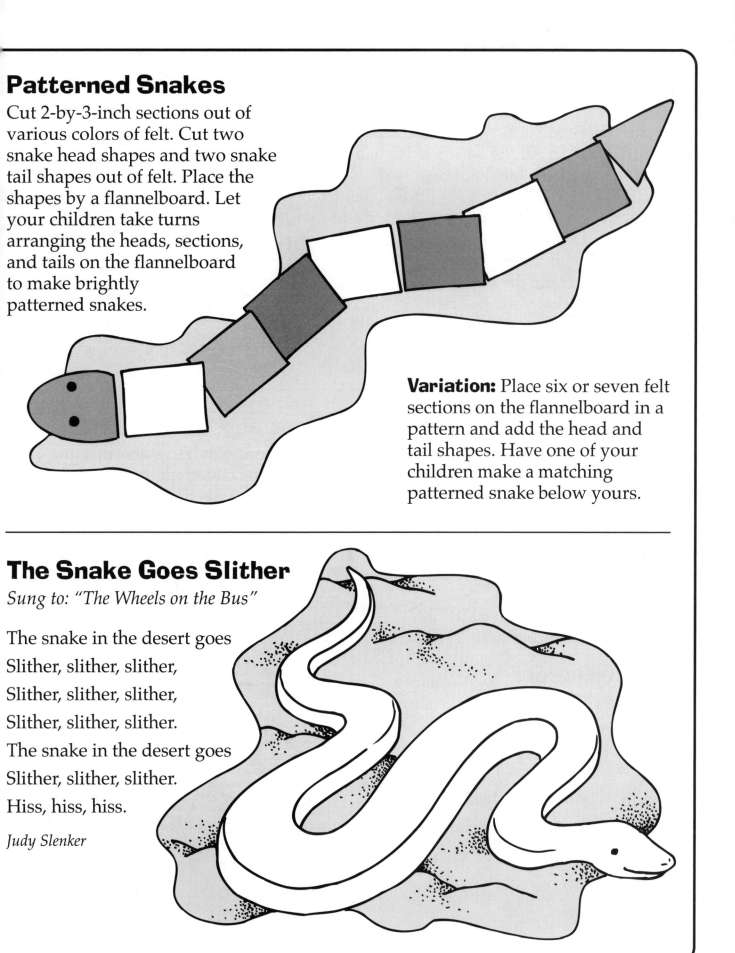

Variation: Place six or seven felt sections on the flannelboard in a pattern and add the head and tail shapes. Have one of your children make a matching patterned snake below yours.

The Snake Goes Slither

Sung to: "The Wheels on the Bus"

The snake in the desert goes
Slither, slither, slither,
Slither, slither, slither,
Slither, slither, slither.
The snake in the desert goes
Slither, slither, slither.
Hiss, hiss, hiss.

Judy Slenker

Desert

Desert Mural

Photocopy the desert animal patterns on pages 91–93. Make as many of each pattern as desired. Cut out the patterns. Place a long piece of blue butcher paper on the floor or a table. Have your children "paint" the bottom half of the paper with glue and then sprinkle on sand to make the desert floor. Shake off the excess sand. Allow the glue to dry. Hang the paper on a wall or a bulletin board at your children's eye level. Let the children attach the desert animal patterns to the paper any way they wish.

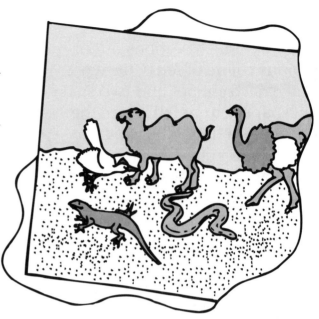

In the Desert

Sung to: "Three Blind Mice"

In the desert, in the desert,
You will find, you will find
Animals both fast and slow,
Ones that run—just watch them go,
Others that crawl just barely so,
In the desert.

Gayle Bittinger

Fast and Slow Game

Have your children stand in a line across one end of an open area. Say the name of a desert animal. If that animal is known for moving quickly, have the children race across the area. If that animal is known for moving slowly, have the children move across the area as slowly as they can. Repeat with other desert animals.

roadrunner

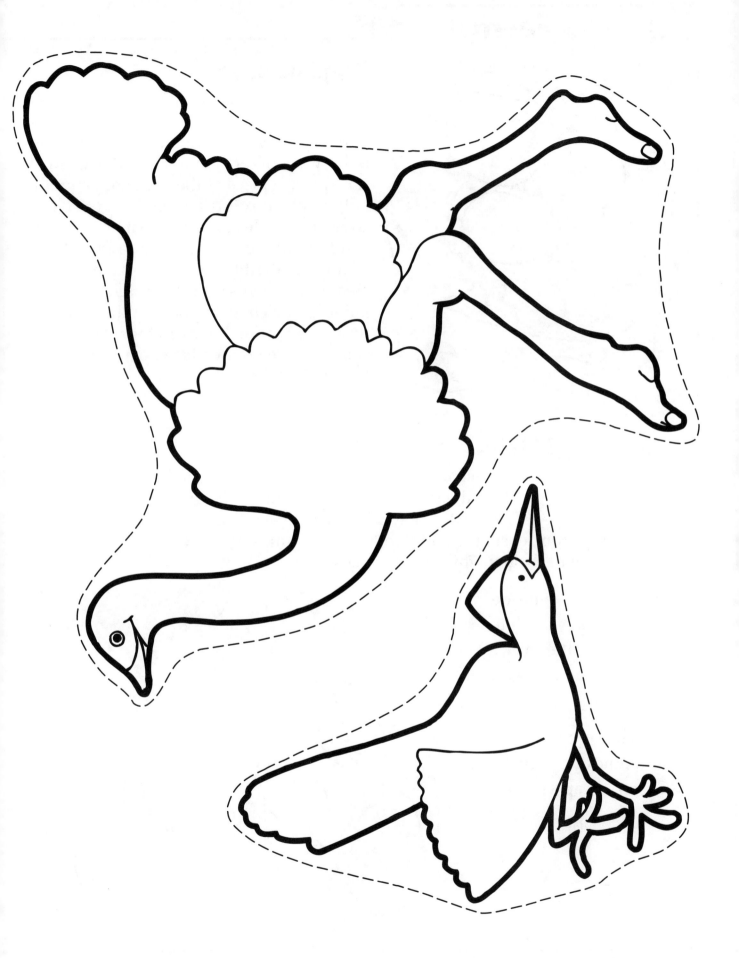

Farm

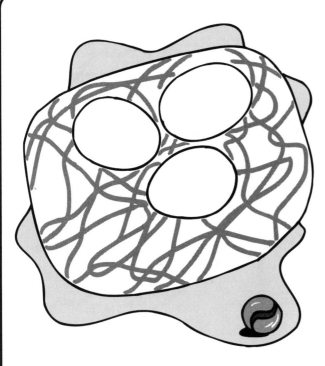

Eggs in Nests

Cut white construction paper that will fit inside sturdy box tops that have been lined with foil. Place marbles in small containers of brown tempera paint. Have one child at a time place a piece of the white paper in the bottom of a box top. Spoon one or two paint-covered marbles onto each paper. Let your children tilt the box tops back and forth, rolling the marbles across their papers to create a criss-cross "nest" design. When the paint has dried, help your children round off the corners of their papers to make nest shapes. Give your children paper egg shapes to glue in their nests.

Hatching Chicks

Have your children crouch down near the floor, pretending to be chicks inside eggs. Have them peck at their pretend shells until the shells break open. Then let the newly hatched "chicks" scamper around the room, cheeping and flapping their wings. If you wish, recite the rhyme below while your "chicks" are hatching.

Snuggled down inside
An egg that was white,
Was a tiny little chick
With its head tucked tight.

Then it tilted its head,
Tapped the egg with its beak,
And quickly popped out.
Cheep, cheep, cheep.

Colraine Pettipaw Hunley

Whose Nest?

Cut five mother hen shapes (see the pattern on page 105), five nest shapes, and fifteen egg shapes out of felt. Number the hens from 1 to 5. Glue a different number of eggs (from 1 to 5) on each nest shape. Place the nests and the mother hens on a flannelboard. Let your children help the mother hens find their nests by counting the eggs and matching each hen to the appropriate nest.

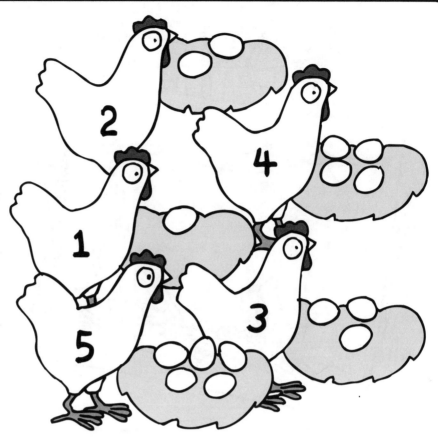

Breakfast Time

Sung to: "Down by the Station"

Down in the barnyard
Early in the morning,
See the little yellow chicks
Standing in a row.
See the busy farmer
Passing out their breakfast.
Cheep, cheep, cheep, cheep,
Off they go.

Jean Warren

Farm

Grazing Cows

Cut cow shapes out of construction paper, using the pattern on page 106 as a guide. Have each of your children glue a cow shape on a sheet of blue construction paper. Talk about what cows eat. Then, with several bottles of glue, take your children outside to a grassy area to pick blades of grass. They can glue them on their pictures.

Variation: Instead of real grass, let your children glue thin strips of green construction paper "grass" on their pictures.

Cow Match

Use the cow pattern on page 106 as a guide for cutting eight cow shapes out of white posterboard. Divide them into four pairs. Use markers to decorate each pair of cows differently. Then mix up the shapes and let your children take turns finding the matching cows.

Leading the Cows Home

With your children, pretend to be cows. Get down on all fours with the children behind you. Then lead them around the room, having them copy your movements. Let your children take turns leading the cows until you finally reach your big barn "home."

Milk the Cow

Let your children pretend to milk a cow while you say the rhyme below.

Milk the cow,
Milk the cow
While sitting on a stool.
Pulling, squirting,
Pulling, squirting,
Till the bucket's full.

Pat Beck

What Do Cows Say?

Sung to: "London Bridge"

What do cows say? Moo, moo, moo;
Moo, moo, moo; moo, moo, moo.
What do cows say? Moo, moo, moo,
Down on the farm.

Additional verses: Cows eat grass and chew, chew, chew; Cows give milk that's true, true, true; I like milk, don't you, you, you?

Becky Valenick

Farm

Horseshoe Prints

Cut a sponge into two horseshoe shapes, and pour tempera paint into shallow containers. Place a piece of butcher paper on the floor or a low table. Let one of your children hold a horseshoe sponge in each hand. Have the child dip the sponges in the paint and then "trot" them across the paper. Let each child have a turn "trotting" the horseshoes. When the paint is dry, hang up the horseshoe art on a wall or a bulletin board.

Horse Story

Ask your children to listen very carefully as you tell a story about horses. Have them neigh whenever you say the word *horse*. Let your children continue the story, stopping to let everyone join them in "neigh" whenever they say the word *horse*.

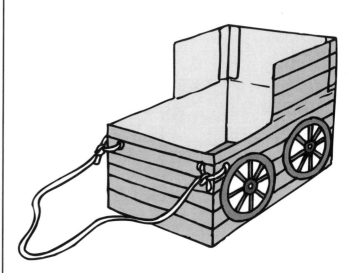

Horse and Wagon

Let your children help you decorate a large cardboard box to look like a wagon. Attach thick yarn to the front of the wagon for a "harness." Let your children pretend to be horses and pull the wagon around the room. Can two children pull the box at the same time? Is it easier or harder with two? Let them put dolls or other toys in the wagon to pull around.

Hobby Horses

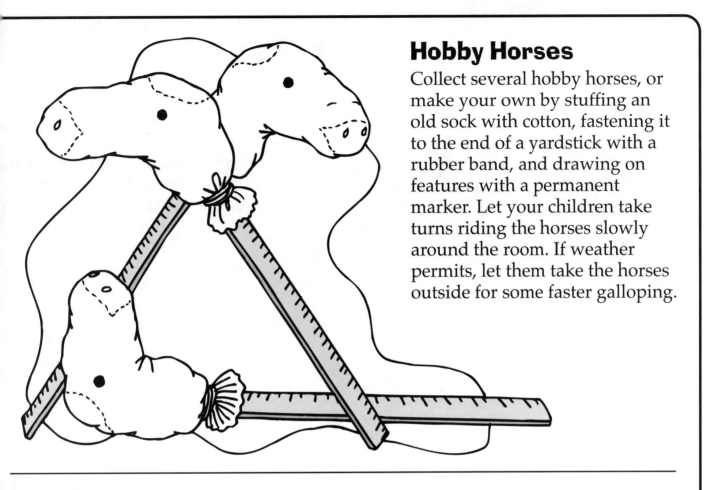

Collect several hobby horses, or make your own by stuffing an old sock with cotton, fastening it to the end of a yardstick with a rubber band, and drawing on features with a permanent marker. Let your children take turns riding the horses slowly around the room. If weather permits, let them take the horses outside for some faster galloping.

My Horse

Sung to: "Twinkle, Twinkle, Little Star"

Trot, trot, trot, my little horse,
Trot, trot, trot, along the course.
Canter, canter, nice and slow,
Canter, canter, off we go.
Gallop, gallop, speed along,
Gallop, gallop to our song.

Carla C. Skjong

Farm

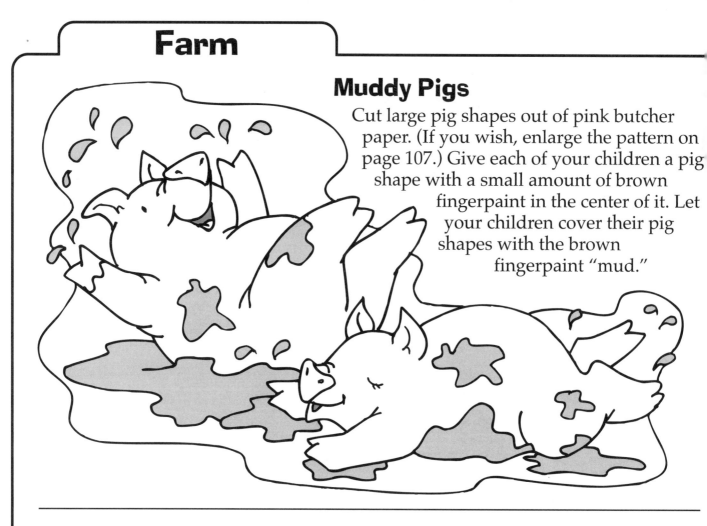

Muddy Pigs

Cut large pig shapes out of pink butcher paper. (If you wish, enlarge the pattern on page 107.) Give each of your children a pig shape with a small amount of brown fingerpaint in the center of it. Let your children cover their pig shapes with the brown fingerpaint "mud."

Looking for Mother

Choose one child to be a baby pig and have that child leave the room with another adult. Ask the remaining children to pretend to be different mother farm animals, including one mother pig. Have the children make their animals' sounds while they walk around the room. Invite the baby pig to return to the room and look and listen for its mother. When the baby animal finds its mother, choose another child to be the baby pig.

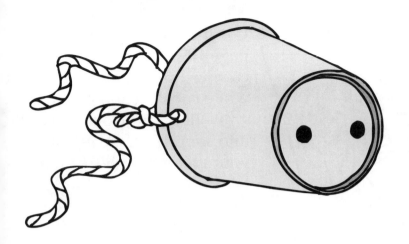

Pig Noses

Give each of your children a plain, white paper cup. Let the children paint their cups pink. When the paint is dry, show them how to use a black marker to add two nostrils to the bottom of the cup to turn it into a Pig Nose. Let them wear their Pig Noses while you sing "In the Mud" below.

In the Mud

Sung to: "Up on the Housetop"

Out in the barnyard
In the mud
Lay the piglets
Nice and smug.
They like to keep cool
From the sun,
So they roll
In the mud for fun.

Oink, oink, oink,
Oh, what fun,
Keeping cool
In the sun.
Three little piglets
Roll and play
In the mud
Most every day.

Jean Warren

Farm

Woolly Sheep

Use the sheep pattern on page 105 as a guide for cutting sheep shapes out of white construction paper. Cut white, tan, and black yarn into short pieces. Give each of your children a sheep shape. Let the children brush glue on their shapes and place the yarn pieces on top of the glue to make Woolly Sheep. Explain that sheep have different colors of fur, or wool, from white to black.

This Little Sheep

Encourage your children to join in as you say and do this finger play.

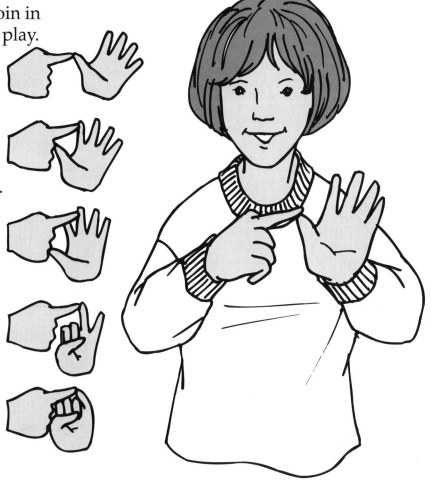

This little sheep eats grass.

> *(Point to thumb.)*

This little sheep likes to play.

> *(Point to index finger.)*

This little sheep drinks water.

> *(Point to middle finger.)*

This little sheep runs away.

> *(Point to ring finger.)*

And this little sheep
 does nothing at all

> *(Point to little finger.)*

But wag its tail all day.

> *(Wiggle little finger.)*

Adapted Traditional

What's Wool?

Collect a variety of samples of sheep's wool, including wool before it's been made into yarn, wool yarn, knitted wool, and wool fabrics. Collect other items with contrasting textures as well. Put all of the items together. Let your children take turns sorting the wool objects from the other ones.

Mary Had a Woolly Lamb

Sung to: "Mary Had a Little Lamb"

Mary had a woolly lamb,
Woolly lamb, woolly lamb.
Mary had a woolly lamb.
Its wool was white as snow.

Its wool was thick and very heavy,
Very heavy, very heavy.
Its wool was thick and very heavy,
So its fleece was sheared.

The wool was soon made into yarn,
Into yarn, into yarn.
The wool was soon made into yarn
And woven into cloth.

Now Mary has a woolly coat,
Woolly coat, woolly coat.
Now Mary has a woolly coat
That she can wear to school.

Jean Warren

Farm

Farm Animal Hunt

Place a piece of butcher paper on the floor. Set out rubber stamps in the shape of farm animals and ink pads. Let your children make prints all over the butcher paper. Give them each a different-colored crayon or marker. Call out the name of one of the animals, such as cows. Let the children search for cows and circle them wherever they find them. Continue until all the animals have been circled.

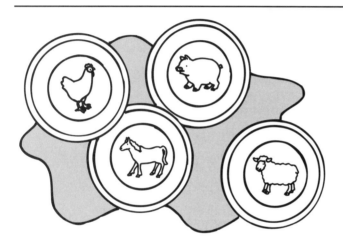

Farm Sounds

Gather several farm animal stickers and the same number of juice can lids. Attach one sticker to each lid. Set the lids facedown on a table. Have your children take turns picking up a lid and making the sound of the animal pictured. Let the rest of the children guess the name of the animal.

Take Me Out to the Barnyard

Sung to: "Take Me Out to the Ball Game"

Take me out to the barnyard.
Take me out there right now.
Show me the cows, pigs, and horses, too.
I hear an "oink" and a "neigh" and
    a "moo."
There are chickens laying their eggs.
If they don't lay, it's a shame.
Oh, it's one, two, three eggs today,
And I'm glad I came.

Judy Hall

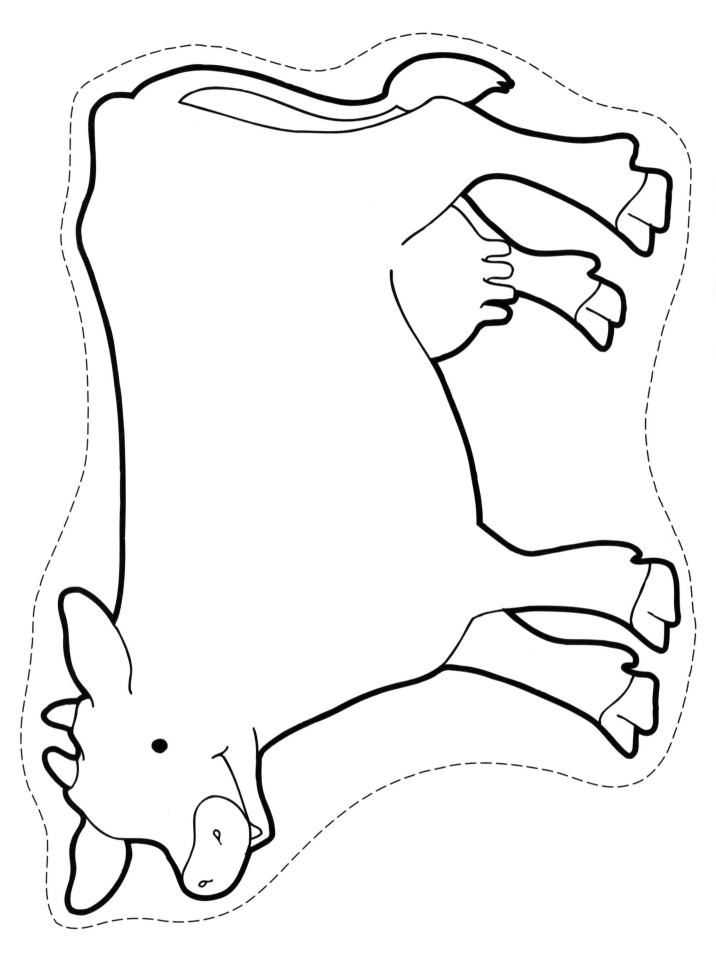

Zoo

Handprint Alligators

Brush the palm of each child's hand with green tempera paint. Then have the child press his or her hand (with fingers together and thumb extended) on a sheet of black construction paper to make an open-jawed "alligator head." Let the child use brushes to paint the alligator's body, tail, and legs with green paint, and its sharp teeth with white paint. Then let the child dip the end of a cork into pink paint and use it to print an eye near the top of the alligator's head.

Cross the River

Make rocks or stepping stones out of large pieces of cardboard or carpet squares. Cut several alligator shapes out of green paper. Place the "rocks" and the "alligators" on the floor. Have your children pretend that most of the floor is a river that is too wide to jump across. Have them leap from one rock to another to get across the river without falling in the water or stepping on one of the alligators.

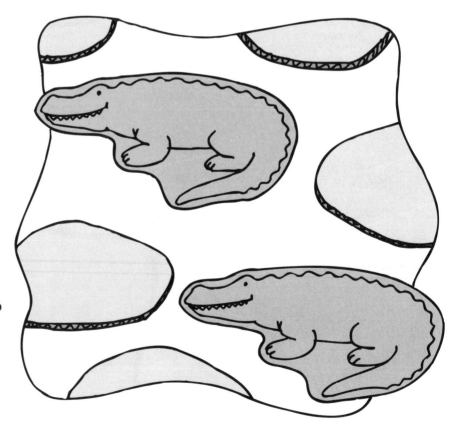

Alligator Puppet Fun

Cut the lids off two egg cartons. Cut jagged teeth around three edges of each lid, leaving one short edge uncut. Put the lids together, with the teeth facing inward, and tape the uncut ends together. Cut two 1-by-6-inch strips out of construction paper. Tape one near the back of the top and bottom lids to make handles. Glue two cotton balls on the top lid, and attach a plastic moving eye to each one. Let the children take turns using the Alligator Puppet while you recite the poem below.

Alligator, alligator, long and green.

Alligator, alligator, teeth so mean.

Snapping at a fly,

Snapping at a bee,

Snapping at a frog,

But you can't catch me!

Jean Warren

bottom ↓

Alligator

Sung to: "Twinkle, Twinkle, Little Star"

Alligator long and green,

You're the meanest thing I've seen.

Sitting on a hollow log,

Trying to catch a big fat frog.

Alligator long and green,

You're the meanest thing I've seen.

Sue Brown

Paper Bag Elephants

For each of your children, cut a paper bag so that it lays flat. Let the children crinkle their bags by grabbing them in different spots and squeezing them. Then have them flatten out their bags and paint them with gray tempera paint. When the paint has dried, cut a large elephant shape out of each child's bag. (Enlarge the pattern on page 125 to use as a guide, if you wish.)

Elephant Puppet

Cut a small circle out of the side of a paper cup to make a nose hole. Add eyes and a mouth with markers. Glue pieces of gray felt or paper cut in the shape of elephants' ears to the sides of the cup. Stick a finger into the cup and out the hole to make an elephant's trunk. Let your children take turns using the Elephant Puppet while you recite the poem below.

Elephant, elephant in the zoo,

I wish I had a trunk like you.

I'd swing it high,

I'd swing it low.

I'd swing it everywhere I go!

Jean Warren

Elephant Walk

Read the poem below out loud while your children act out the motions.

Right foot, left foot, see me go.

> *(Put weight on one foot then the other, swaying from side to side.)*

I am gray and big and slow.

> *(Walk slowly around the room.)*

I come walking down the street
With my trunk and four big feet.

> *(Extend arms together in front and swing them like a trunk.)*

Author Unknown

Big and Gray

Sung to: "The Mulberry Bush"

Elephants are big and gray,
Big and gray, big and gray.
Elephants swing their trunks this way,
Back and forth all day.

Carla C. Skjong

Zoo

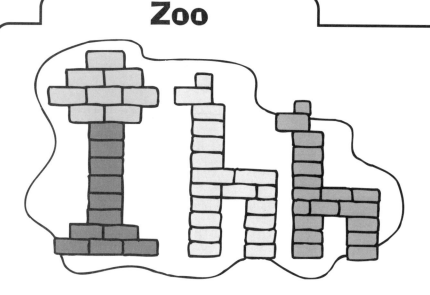

Giraffe Blocks

Set out a box of large, interlocking blocks. Let your children use the blocks to make giraffes with long necks. Encourage them to make mother and father giraffes and baby giraffes. Let them make block trees for the giraffes to nibble on.

Giraffe Magnet Game

Turn a plain paper cup on its side. Tape a strong magnet to the bottom of the cup. Use markers to draw a giraffe's features on the cup (see illustration). Use a sharp knife to cut an X on the bottom side of the cup for a finger hole. Cut leaf shapes out of green construction paper. Fashion paper clips into S shapes and put one on each leaf. String a length of yarn between two chairs, and hang the leaves on it. Let your children take turns being the giraffe. Have them put the giraffe cup on their index finger and pretend that their arm is the giraffe's neck. Let them use the magnet on the end of the giraffe's nose to unhook the leaves for "eating."

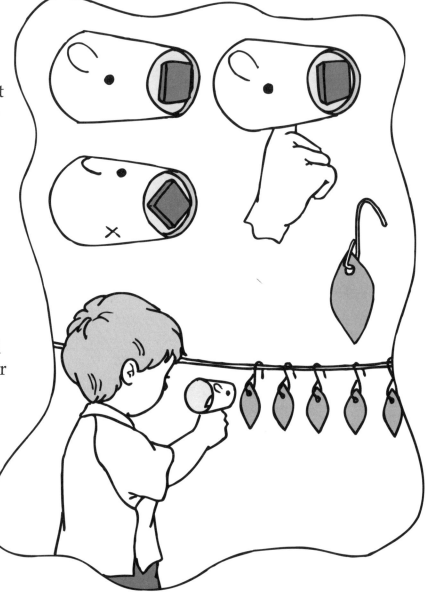

Giraffe Friends

Collect several plastic toy giraffes. Set out the giraffes along with yellow modeling dough. Point out giraffes' long necks to your children. Let them use the modeling dough to make long-necked friends for the giraffes.

Long-Necked Giraffe

Sung to: "Three Blind Mice"

Long-necked giraffe,
Long-necked giraffe,
You make me laugh,
You make me laugh.
It's true you can reach
The highest tree,
But it's hard bending down
To talk to me,
'Cause your neck is too long
For your body,
Long-necked giraffe.

Susan M. Paprocki

Zoo

Lion Art

Cut yellow crepe paper into short strips. Set out the crepe-paper strips, paper plates, glue in shallow containers, brushes, and crayons. Let your children brush glue around the edge of their plates. Then have them place the crepe-paper strips on the glue to make a lion's "mane." Once the glue has dried, let your children add facial features with the crayons.

Roar Like a Lion

To play this game, hold up one of the Lion Art plates from the activity above. When your children see the "lion," have them roar. Hide the plate away, and have the children stop roaring. Hold up the plate again, and have the children roar. Repeat several times. Encourage your children to watch carefully and to start and stop as soon as possible.

On the Savanna

Let your children create an environment for lions at the sand table. Set out a variety of props including toy plastic lions, rocks, grass (either clumps of real grass or plastic aquarium grass), and model trees (simple ones made from cardboard tubes and green paper or ready-made ones from a hobby or craft store). Let your children play with the lions while they make an open grassland or lightly wooded savanna habitat for them.

Act Like Lions

Sung to: "Skip to My Lou"

Act, act, act like lions.
Act, act, act like lions.
Act, act, act like lions.
Let's see and hear those lions.

Run, run, run like lions.
Run, run, run like lions.
Run, run, run like lions.
Run across the plains.

Roar, roar, roar like lions.
Roar, roar, roar like lions.
Roar, roar, roar like lions.
Roar all through the day!

Cindy Dingwall

Zoo

Monkeys See, Monkeys Do

Have your children stand in a circle and pretend to be monkeys. Choose one child to make a movement, and have the other children try to imitate it. Say the rhyme below, substituting the name of the movement the child has chosen for *jump*. Continue reciting the rhyme until all the children have been chosen to lead a movement.

Monkeys, monkeys in the tree.
Can you jump around like me?
Monkeys see, monkeys do,
Little monkeys in the zoo.

Jean Warren

Banana Count

Cut a monkey shape out of brown felt, using the monkey pattern on page 124 as a guide. Place the shape on a flannelboard. Cut 5 to 10 banana shapes out of yellow felt and put them in a pile. Let your children take turns "feeding the monkey" by placing banana shapes on the flannelboard. As they do so, count the bananas with the group.

Extension: Give your "monkeys" real banana halves to eat at snacktime.

I'm a Little Monkey

Let your children pretend to be monkeys and act out the motions as you say the rhyme below out loud.

I'm a little monkey.
Watch me play.
    (Hop around.)
Munching on bananas
Every day.
    (Pretend to eat.)
I have monkey friends
Who play with me.
    (Point to others.)
See us climb
Right up the tree!
    (Pretend to climb.)

Carla C. Skjong

Did You Ever See a Monkey?

Sung to: "Did You Ever See a Lassie?"

Did you ever see a monkey,
A monkey, a monkey?
Did you ever see a monkey
Swing high in the trees?
Jumping and leaping,
With antics so pleasing,
Did you ever see a monkey
Swing high in the trees?

Bev Qualheim

Zoo

Fingerprint Penguins

Pour some thick, black paint into a shallow container. Have your children dip their fingers into the paint and make fingerprints on white paper. When the paint is dry, outline each black print with a black fine point marker and add legs and facial features to turn the prints into penguins.

Floating Penguins

To make buoyant penguins for water play, draw black faces and bodies on white Ping-Pong balls (use waterproof ink). Add ice cubes to turn your water table (or a dishpan full of water) into an Antarctic playground.

Penguin Pals

Collect a 4-inch length of cardboard tube for each of your children. Have the children paint the cardboard tubes with black tempera paint. Allow the tubes to dry overnight. The next day, have each child attach a wide strip of white tape, lengthwise, to his or her painted tube to give the penguins a white front. Provide markers for making eyes and beaks.

Extension: Cover wooden blocks with white socks to make "snow blocks." Encourage your children to use the white blocks to build a habitat for their penguins.

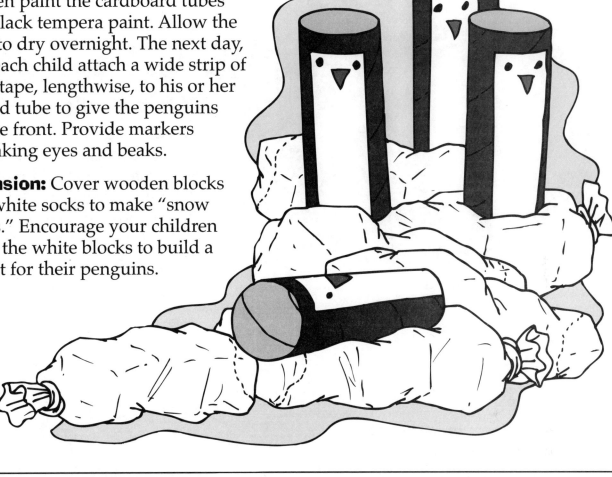

Romp and Play

Sung to: "Twinkle, Twinkle, Little Star"

Watch the penguins romp and play,
Sliding on the ice all day.
Dressed in coats of black and white,
They are such a funny sight.
Watch the penguins as they play,
On a cold, cold winter day.

Pat Beck

Zoo

Zebra Mask

Cut eye holes out of a paper plate. Leave the front of the paper plate white and paint the back with vertical black stripes. Glue on nose and ear shapes and add tissue paper strips around the edge of the plate. Attach a tongue depressor handle for a child to hold the mask in front of his or her face.

Zebra Prints

Cut an assortment of large and small shapes from corrugated cardboard. Have your children lay thin pieces of paper over the cardboard shapes and rub a black crayon over the paper. Stripes will appear like magic, making Zebra Prints.

Black and White

Hang a large sheet of white paper on your easel. Set out thick black paint. Show your children how to paint black stripes up and down or across the paper. Let each child have a turn making black stripes on a clean sheet of white paper.

Variation: Hang a large sheet of black paper on your easel and let your children add white painted stripes to it.

Stripes From Head to Toe

Sung to: "Jingle Bells"

Zebra black, zebra white,
Stripes from head to toe.
What a special animal
For everyone to know.
Zebra black, zebra white,
Stripes from head to toe.
What a special animal
For everyone to know.

Betty Silkunas

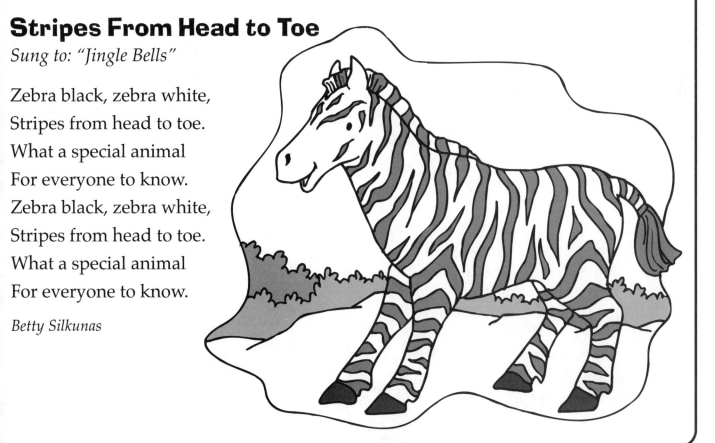

Zoo

Zoo Puzzles

Photocopy two to four zoo animal patterns found on pages 124–127. Cut a square out of heavy paper for each one. Glue an animal pattern to each square. Divide each square into three or four squares or horizontal or vertical strips. Put a short length of magnetic strip on the back of each puzzle piece. Mix up the pieces and let your children take turns putting the puzzles together on a metal surface.

Zoo Hokey-Pokey

Have your children sing and move like their favorite zoo animals while doing the Hokey-Pokey. Let the children take turns picking out an animal to imitate and the part of the animal's body to sing about. For example, "You shake your lion's mane in; You stick your giraffe neck in; You snap your alligator jaws in; You swing your monkey arms in."

Zoo Mural

Use markers to draw a simple zoo background scene on a large sheet of paper. For example, you might include pictures of rocks, grass, trees, and a stream. Place the paper on a low table or on the floor. Provide colored ink pads and rubber stamps in the shape of zoo animals. Have your children ink the stamps and then press them all over the zoo background scene. Display the completed mural on a wall or a bulletin board.

The Zoo Story

Share the story below with your children. Pause as you come to each blank, and give them a chance to fill it in.

I love the zoo.

There are so many animals to see.

The silliest animal is the _____.

The tallest animal is the _____.

The smallest animal is the _____.

The friendliest animal is the _____.

The fattest animal is the _____.

The noisiest animal is the _____.

The cleanest animal is the _____.

The prettiest animal is the _____.

My favorite animal is the _____.

If I had room, I would keep a _____ in my yard.

Jean Warren

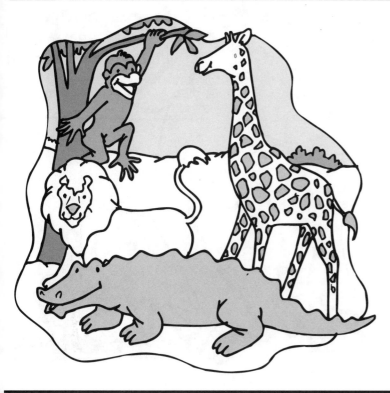

Going to the Zoo

Sung to: "Yankee Doodle"

If you're going to the zoo,
Remember who will meet you.
Giraffes, zebras, alligators,
And monkeys, they will greet you.
Next, you'll see the king of all,
And lion is his name.
The penguins and elephants
Will all be glad you came.

Judy Hall

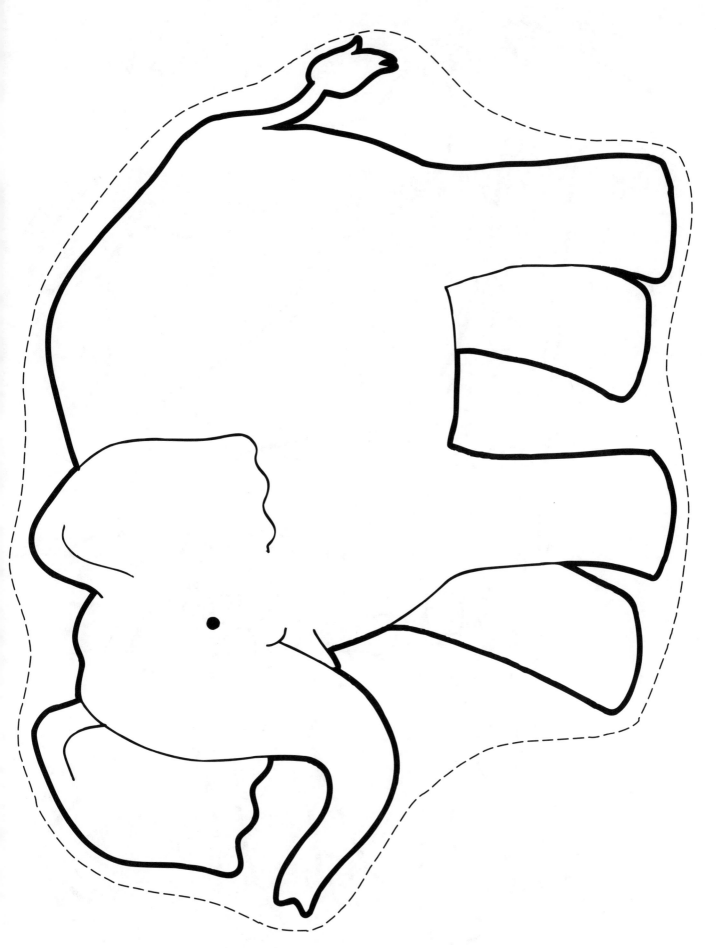

Pets

Cat Names

Cut out several pictures of cats. Glue each picture to a separate sheet of paper to create posters. Show the posters to your children. Have them look carefully at each cat's picture and think up names that match its appearance or personality. For example, if you showed them a picture of a black cat, they might think of the names Licorice or Midnight. Write the names they think up on each cat's poster.

Where's the Mouse?

Cut several oval mouse shapes out of gray construction paper. Hide the "mice" around your room. Let your children pretend to be cats and hunt for the mice. Encourage them to move on all fours like cats, purring and meowing as they search. If necessary, give them clues about where the mice are hidden.

Cat Moves

Have your children pretend to be cats sleeping on the floor. Have them wake up, stretch, then pretend to wash their faces with their paws. Hold a pretend toy on a string above the cats and let them jump and swat at it. When the cats become sleepy, have them roll over, curl up, and go back to sleep again.

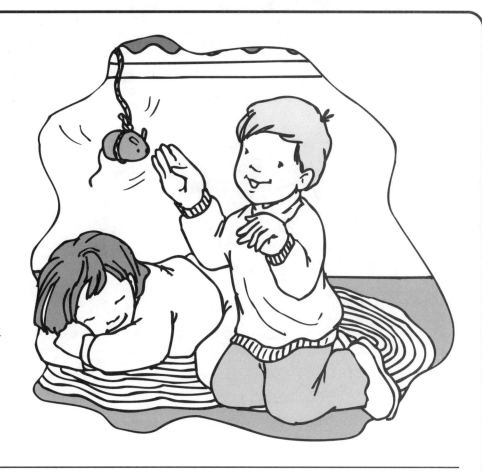

My Kitten

Sung to: "Sing a Song of Sixpence"

I have a little kitten,
She's black and white and gray.
When I try to cuddle her,
She always wants to play.
So I drag a piece of yarn
Across the kitchen floor.
She thinks it is a little mouse
To chase right out the door.

Elizabeth Vollrath

Pets

In the Doghouse

Make a house for a toy dog by turning a cardboard carton upside down and cutting a large door in one side. Let your children decorate the doghouse with stickers and crayons. Place the doghouse, along with the toy dog, on the floor. Let the children take turns playing with the dog, moving it in and out of its house. If desired, add a dog dish and dog toys, such as a ball or a rawhide bone.

Digging Up Bones

Hide several dog bones or blocks in a sandbox or dishpan filled with sand. Let your children pretend to be dogs while they dig through the sand to find the bones. Encourage them to really dig around to find every bone. If you wish, tell them how many bones are hidden, so they can find each one.

Puppy Moves

Let your children pretend to be puppies. Recite the rhyme below and have your children act out the motions indicated. Repeat several times, substituting a different phrase, such as *roll around, jump up high,* or *sniff your nose,* for *wag your tail.*

Puppy, puppy,
Watch when I say "Go!"
Puppy, puppy,
Wag your tail just so.

Jean Warren

Three Little Puppies
Sung to: "Ten Little Indians"

One little, two little,
Three little puppy dogs,
One little, two little,
Three little puppy dogs,
One little, two little,
Three little puppy dogs
Bark like this all day.

Additional verses: Substitute the names of other things puppy dogs do such as *play, eat,* or *sleep* for *bark.*

Carla C. Skjong

Pets

Pet Goldfish

Bring in a goldfish, a fishbowl, aquarium gravel, and some aquarium plants. Let your children help you set up the fishbowl for the goldfish. Place the bowl in a safe spot where the children can observe the fish swimming around in it. Encourage discussion of the parts of the fish and how it moves. If desired, let the children help with the feeding. (Note: Check with a pet store or an aquarium store for the proper way to set up your fishbowl and care for your fish.)

I'm a Goldfish

Sung to: "Clementine"

I'm a goldfish,
I'm a goldfish.
See me wave
My fins like this.
> *(Wave arms at sides.)*

See me swim round
In my fishbowl.
> *(Move in a circle.)*

See my tail go
Swish, swish, swish.
> *(Wiggle hips.)*

Elizabeth McKinnon

Swimming Fish

Arrange a long piece of yarn on the floor in a circle to represent a fishbowl. Let your children take turns pretending to be goldfish swimming around inside it.

Rabbit Jump

Place small pillows on a carpeted floor or outside on the grass. Ask your children to pretend to be rabbits. Have them hold their hands by their ears for long "bunny ears." Then have your "bunnies" practice their bunny hops by jumping over and around all the pillows.

My Rabbit

Sung to: "London Bridge"

Rabbit's fur is soft and white,
Soft and white, soft and white.
Rabbit's fur is soft and white,
What a sight!

Rabbit's ears flop high and low,
High and low, high and low.
Rabbit's ears flop high and low,
Watch them go!

Bonnie Woodard

Pets

Pets and Owners

Have half of your children pretend to be pet owners and let the other half pretend to be pets. Have the owners do pretend activities such as feeding, walking, petting, and playing with their pets. Then let the children reverse roles.

Pet Day

Plan a Pet Day with your children. Invite them to bring in their pets—or photos of their pets—for others to see. Give each child a chance to talk about his or her pet and to tell how he or she helps care for it.

Our Pet

Make copies of the pet patterns on pages 136–137. Let each child choose one to decorate and glue onto a sheet of construction paper. Write the chosen name for each child's pet. Let the children tell about their pets after repeating this rhyme after you.

Our pet has
A special place.
We keep it clean
And neat.
We feed our pet
Every day.
It sure likes
To eat!

Cindy Dingwall

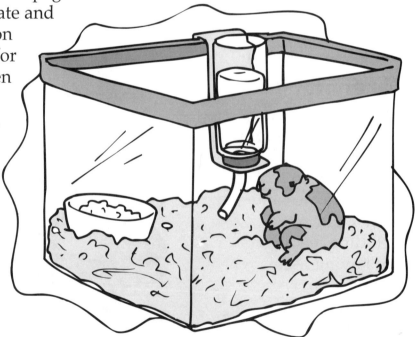

Pet Survey

Divide a piece of white paper by drawing four horizontal lines, two inches apart. Label the top of the paper "Pet Survey." Draw a picture at the beginning of each line to represent different kinds of pets. Attach the piece of paper to a clipboard and let your children survey classmates, friends, neighbors, etc. Have them place a check mark in the appropriate area when someone says he or she has a certain pet. Help them look at their results and discuss them.

Love Your Pets

Talk about the things pets need every day to keep healthy and strong, such as food, water, exercise, rest, and lots of love. Then sing the song below with your children.

Sung to: "Row, Row, Row Your Boat"

Love, love, love your pets,
Love them every day.
Give them food and water, too,
Then let them run and play.

Elizabeth McKinnon

Veterinarian Visit

Invite a veterinarian or veterinary worker to visit. Arrange for him or her to bring a kitten or puppy to show your group. Ask your visitor to show the children the proper way to hold and play with the animal. Have the visitor discuss pet care, including feeding, grooming, exercising, and having regular checkups. If possible, arrange to have your visitor show the children some pet supplies such as a feeding dish, a collar, and a few toys.

Bugs

Honeybee Movement

Ask your children to pretend that your room is a beehive and that they are all honeybees. As the queen or king bee, you will assign tasks to your worker bees. Make up beehive tasks that require large physical movements. For example, have some workers pour the nectar from flowers into pails, have others stir the nectar in a big pot to make honey, and have the rest sweep the hive. Before your busy bees have tired, appoint different children to take turns being the queen or king bee and to make up other imaginative jobs for the workers.

The Bee Song

Have your children name parts of their bodies where an imaginary bee might land. Substitute those names for *nose*.

Sung to: "The Farmer in the Dell"

The bee is on my nose,
The bee is on my nose,
It's right on me, just look and see,
The bee is on my nose.

Jean Warren

Bumblebee Clip-Ons

For each of your children, cut a bumblebee body shape, about 3½ inches long, from yellow construction paper. Let the children draw black crayon stripes on their shapes and glue on wing shapes cut from white tissue paper. Then have them glue their bee shapes onto unpainted clothespins. Let them clip their bees all around the room. Or, use the bees as you and your children sing "The Bee Song" (see left).

Butterflies

Let each of your children flatten a paper baking cup and decorate it with crayons or markers. Show the children how to make a butterfly shape by pinching together the center of the flattened cup. Then help each child twist a pipe cleaner around the pinched center and curl the ends to resemble antennae.

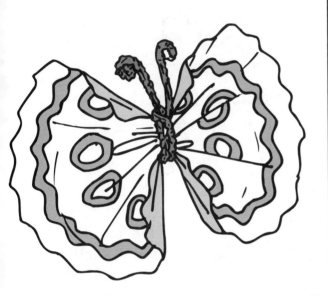

Butterfly Catcher

Cut butterfly shapes out of lightweight paper. (Use the pattern on page 145 as a guide, if you wish.) Throw them up into the air and let your children take turns catching them with a strainer.

Flutter, Flutter

Sung to: "Twinkle, Twinkle, Little Star"

Flutter, flutter, butterfly,
Floating in the summer sky.
Floating by for all to see,
Floating by so merrily.
Flutter, flutter, butterfly,
Floating in the summer sky.

Bonnie Woodard

Creeping Caterpillar

Cut all twelve egg cups out of an egg carton. Poke a hole in the bottom of each cup and string the cups on a piece of yarn to make a "caterpillar." (Add facial features to one end.) Tie knots in both ends of the yarn. Cut another piece of yarn and tie one end to the knot at the front of the caterpillar and the other end to the yarn near the eighth egg cup. Make the caterpillar crawl by holding onto the loop of yarn and moving it up and down.

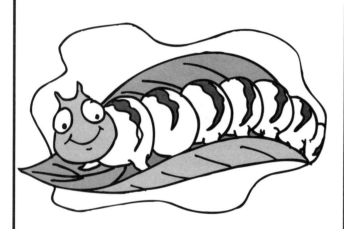

Caterpillar, Caterpillar

Sung to: "Jingle Bells"

Caterpillar, caterpillar,
Creeping right by me.
You will find some leafy greens
In that nearby tree.
Caterpillar, caterpillar,
Spin your cocoon tight.
Soon you'll be a butterfly
And fly by—what a sight!

Gayle Bittinger

Caterpillar Mural

Give each of your children a small paper plate. Have the children decorate their plates with crayons or markers. On another plate, draw a caterpillar face and glue on construction paper or pipe cleaner antennae. Attach a small piece of magnetic strip to the back of each plate. Arrange the plates (starting with the face) in a curvy line on a large metal surface, such as a refrigerator, to make a Caterpillar Mural.

Variation: Omit the magnets and hang the plates in a curvy line on a wall or a bulletin board.

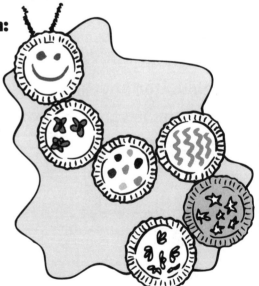

Ladybug Spots

Using the pattern on page 146, cut five ladybug shapes out of red paper. Number the ladybugs from 1 to 5. Place the appropriate number of small round magnets on each ladybug and trace around them. Remove the magnets. Attach the shapes to a nonaluminum baking sheet with removable poster-mounting tape or double-sided masking tape. Set out the baking sheet and 15 round magnets. Let your children take turns putting the appropriate number of magnet "spots" on each ladybug.

I'm a Little Ladybug

Have your children use their fingers as ladybugs to act out the movements suggested in the song.

Sung to: "I'm a Little Teapot"

I'm a little ladybug on the go,
Landing on an arm, now an elbow.
See me fly round and round your hand,
Now watch as on your thumb I land.

I'm a little ladybug searching for some toes,
But watch me quickly land on your nose.
Now I look around and head for your hair,
I muss it up a bit, then pat it down with care.

I'm a little ladybug looking for a knee,
I'm just so happy you're not bugged by me.
Now you see me heading for your chest,
This little ladybug needs some rest.

Susan M. Paprocki

Bugs

Spider Webs

Cut 6-inch squares out of white cardboard and make five to six slits around each edge. Tape a piece of black yarn to the back of each square and pull it through one of the slits. Have your children cross the yarn back and forth over the fronts of their cardboard squares, attaching it through the slits (slits can be used more than once). Let them continue until their squares resemble spider webs. When the children are finished, trim the ends of their yarn and tape them to the backs of their squares.

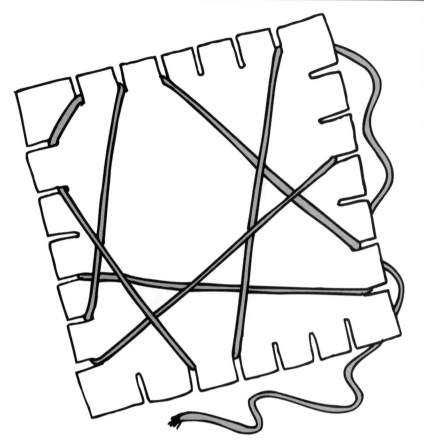

Spider Prints

For each of your children, make a copy of the spider web pattern on page 147. Set out a black ink pad and let your children make fingerprints on their web shapes. Show them how to use a black marker to draw eight legs and two eyes on each fingerprint to make spiders.

Extension: Let your children count the number of "spiders" on each web for you to write on the bottom.

Spider Day

Plan a Spider Day with your children. Bring in a black spider for them to examine and observe. Talk about what spiders do and how they can be distinguished from insects (spiders have eight legs; insects have six). At the end of the day, go outside with the children and set the spider free.

The Teeny Tiny Spider

Read the rhyme below out loud to your children. Have them pretend their fingers are the spider in the poem and crawl along with him.

The teeny tiny spider
Began to crawl on me.
I found him on my leg,
To be exact, my knee.

The teeny tiny spider
Crawled up to my chest.
This was such a long trip,
He took a little rest.

The teeny tiny spider
Headed for my arm.
It tickled quite a bit,
But I knew he meant no harm.

The teeny tiny spider
Crawled up on my finger.
He landed on my thumb,
But he didn't want to linger.

I helped him to my face
And placed him on my nose.
Then he lost his balance
And fell down to my toes.

The teeny tiny spider
Went upon his way.
He'd clearly had enough
Of his crawling for today.

Susan M. Paprocki

Bugs

Bug Investigation

Insects fascinate children. Take advantage of this natural curiosity and help your children collect four or five different bugs for observation. Look for differences and similarities among your specimens. Are they big or small? Do they have wings? How many legs do they have? Are all insect bodies divided into three parts? When you finish your investigation, remember to return your specimens outdoors.

Found a Bug

Make several copies of each of the patterns on page 145. Cut out each bug shape and place it around the room. Begin singing the first verse of the song below. Have your children hunt for the bug shapes. When a bug is found, sing the second verse, substituting the name of the bug that was found for *bumblebee.*

Sung to: "Found a Peanut"

Found a bug, found a bug,
Found a bug right here.
Right here, I found a bug,
Found a bug right here.

It's a bumblebee, it's a bumblebee,
It's a bumblebee right here.
Right here, I found a bumblebee,
Found a bumblebee right here.

Gayle Bittinger

Right here, I found a bumblebee, Found a bumblebee right here.

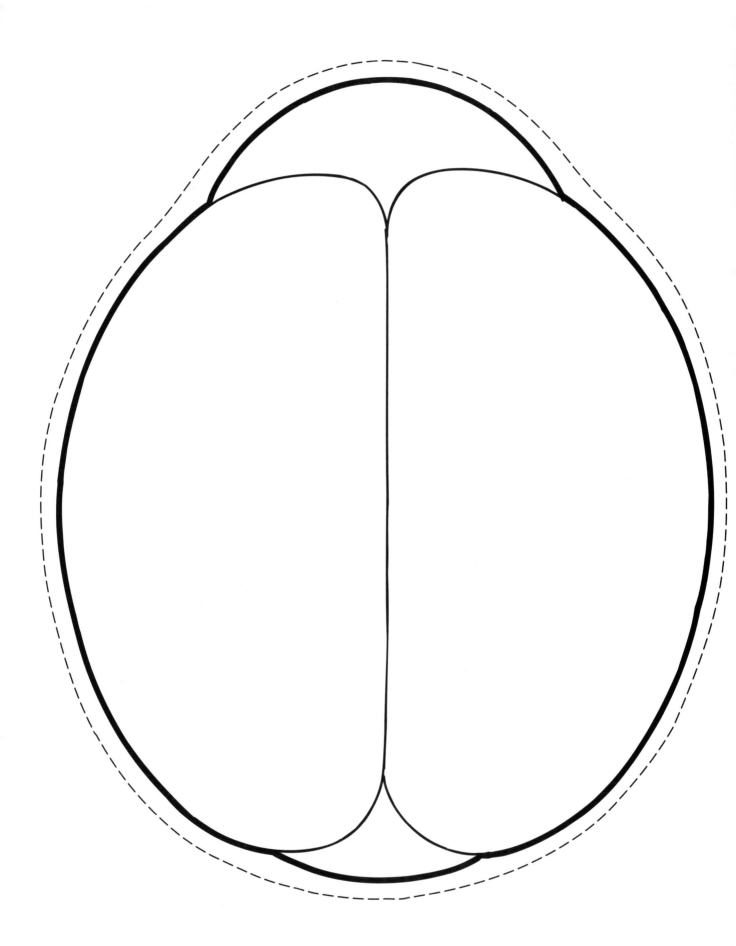

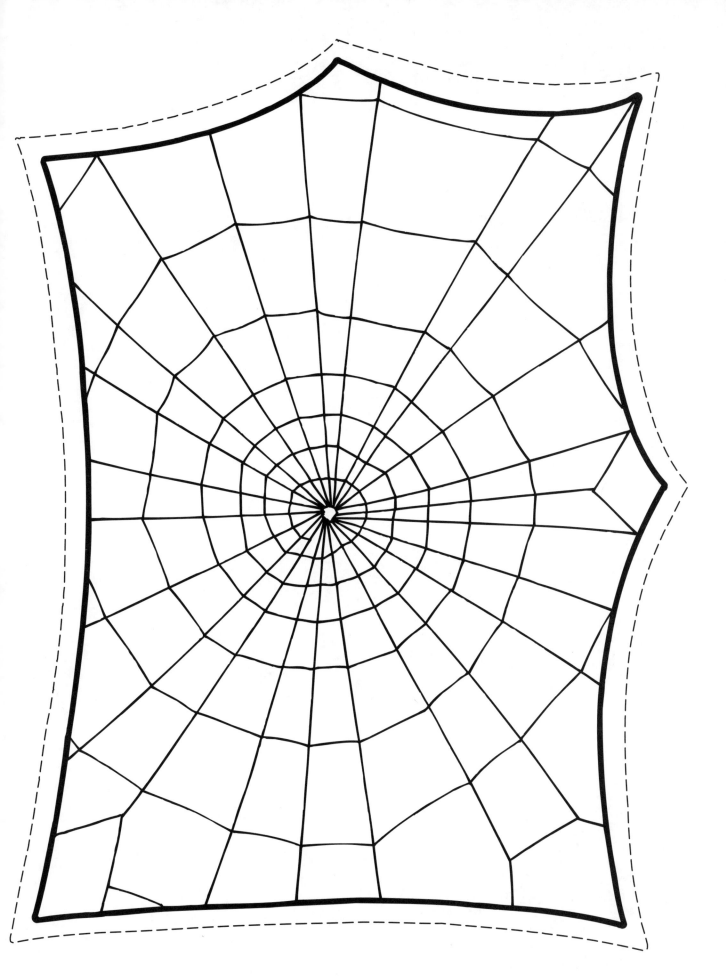

Plants and Food

Plants

Leaf Prints

Go outside with your children and take pieces of plain white paper, crayons, and a hard surface to color on, such as a baking sheet. Ask your children to search for interesting plants. When they find one, have them carefully put one of the leaves or branches of the plant between a sheet of paper and the hard surface and rub the crayon over it. Have your children collect rubbings of several different kinds of plants. Ask them to describe how the plants are alike and how they are different.

Seed Mosaics

Show and discuss with your children various kinds of seeds. Explain that almost all plants start as tiny seeds. Then set out bowls of different kinds of seeds, glue, brushes, and pieces of paper. Have the children brush glue on the paper. Then let them arrange seeds on the glue to create Seed Mosaics.

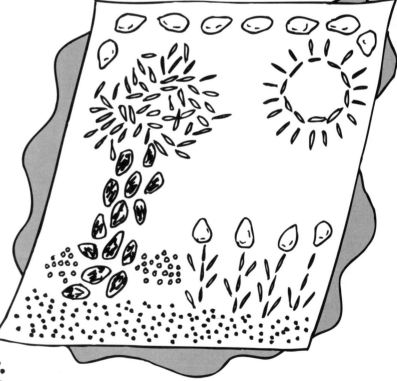

Tin Can Planters

Use a can opener to completely remove one end from each of several tin cans. Check the rims of the cans for rough edges, and cover them with masking tape, if necessary. Set out the cans, glue, and decorating materials (yarn, fabric scraps, self-stick paper, construction paper, crayons, etc.). Fill a small watering can with water. Let your children use the decorating materials to decorate their cans any way they wish. When they have finished, have them each put a layer of small rocks or gravel in the bottoms of their cans. Then let them add dirt. Give each child several flower seeds or seedlings. Set the planters by a sunny window. Have your children use the watering can to water their seeds or seedlings as needed. Encourage them to check regularly for signs of growth.

Egg Carton Nursery

Place empty eggshell halves in the cups of an egg carton. Let your children fill the shells with potting soil and carefully plant one or two lettuce or carrot seeds in each one. Have them add a teaspoon of water to each shell. Keep the egg carton closed so that the seeds will stay warm and sprout more quickly, watering the soil as necessary to keep it moist. After the seeds have sprouted and grown into seedlings, have the children plant the eggshells outside, crushing them slightly before placing them in the ground.

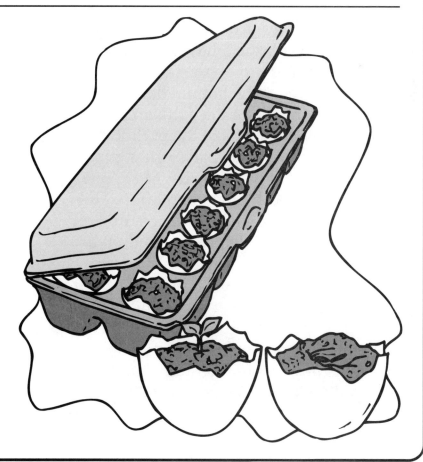

Plants

Individual Terrariums

Have each of your children fill a clear-plastic cup half full with dirt. Let the children plant small plants in the dirt, cover the dirt with wood chips or rocks, and sprinkle on a little water. Place another clear-plastic cup over each child's planted cup and glue or tape them together. Explain to your children that terrariums water themselves. Encourage them to watch over the next few days how the water condenses on the top of their terrariums and "rains" down on their plants.

Plastic-Bottle Terrariums

To make each terrarium, cut the top half off an empty, plastic 1-liter soft-drink bottle. Keep the cap on the bottle. (Recycle or reuse the bottom half of the bottle.) Set the top of the bottle in an aluminum pie pan. Glue the perimeter of the bottle to the pie pan (a glue gun works well). Let the glue dry. Make one terrarium for each of your children. Then have your children take the caps off their terrarium bottles. Help your children use funnels to put dirt through the tops of the bottles into the pans. Then have your children drop in flower seeds and use the funnels to put more dirt on top of the seeds. Have your children add small amounts of water to their terrariums and put the caps back on. Place the terrariums in a sunny place.

My Plants

Read the rhyme below out loud to your children. Let them act out the motions.

I rake, and I hoe.
And I dig, dig, dig,
To plant my
Garden row.
The sun will shine
And the rain will fall,
And my plants
Will grow and grow!

Margo S. Miller

Is It From a Plant?

Collect a variety of wood, paper, cotton, and food products (nuts and seeds). Lay everything out and let your children guess which items come from a plant. Have them keep guessing and choosing until everything is identified as a plant product. Nobody will ever be wrong, but they will all be very surprised!

Plants

Seed Sorter

Collect six different-looking types of seeds. Mix up the seeds on a tray. Let your children take turns sorting the seeds into a muffin tin. Have them notice the differences and similarities between the seeds. Can they guess what plants the seeds will grow into?

Seeds Are Strong

Completely fill a small plastic container with bean seeds or dried beans such as kidney beans. Add water to the top of the container and put on the lid. Leave the container out overnight. Ask your children to guess what will happen to the bean seeds and the container. (The lid will pop off because the seeds will absorb the water and begin to swell and sprout.)

Plants Need Water

Place two identical houseplants that need frequent watering in a window. Let your children take turns watering just one of the plants. After several days, have them compare the plants. Which plant looks healthy? Which plant looks droopy? Can they name one thing that plants need to grow? Now let the children water both of the plants until they both look healthy.

What Do Plants Need?

Sung to: "The Mulberry Bush"

Little plant, oh, what do you need,
What do you need, what do you need?
Little plant, oh, what do you need,
To grow up big and strong?

I need water to stand up tall,
Stand up tall, stand up tall.
I need water to stand up tall,
To grow up big and strong.

I need sun to make my food,
Make my food, make my food.
I need sun to make my food,
To grow up big and strong.

Jean Warren

Plants Need Light

Set out two identical houseplants that need lots of sunlight. Have your children help you place one of the plants by a sunny window and the other plant in a dark place, such as a closet or a cabinet. Let the children take turns watering both plants. After a while, set the two plants out on a table. Ask the children to describe the differences in the plants. Why does one of the plants look unhealthy? What could they do to make it healthy again? What is something plants need to grow?

Plants

Parts of a Plant

About a week before doing this activity, fill a clear-plastic cup with dirt and plant a few bean seeds in it, close to one side. Water the seeds as necessary. Photocopy the bean plant picture on page 159. Cut the picture in three puzzle pieces, each one with a different plant part on it. Show your children one of the bean plants growing in the cup. Help them name the different parts of the plant, including the roots, which should be visible through the side of the cup. Then set out the puzzle pieces and let the children take turns putting the puzzle together and identifying the roots, stem, and leaves.

Hint: If the roots of the plants do not show through the side of the cup, gently remove one of the plants for the demonstration and replant it later.

Plants Everywhere

Plants help keep our air clean. They take in carbon dioxide and produce oxygen that people and animals breathe. Take your children on a walk outside. How many different kinds of plants can they find? Which one is the tallest? The shortest? How many different colors of plants do they see? If you have plants indoors, have your children observe and count them as well.

Gardening in Rows

Let your children plant seeds in their own garden "rows." Remove the lids from several cardboard egg cartons and save them for another use. Cut the bottoms of the egg cartons in half lengthwise to create rows. Give each child one row. Let the children fill the egg cups in their rows with potting soil. Have them plant fast-growing seeds, such as sunflower, radish, or marigold seeds, in the dirt. From time to time, ask your children to tell you how their gardens are growing.

Plants and Seeds

Planting Seeds

When planting seeds with your children, let them help you make a display of the seeds you are using and the plants they will become. Glue a few of each kind of seed in a column on the left-hand side of a sheet of posterboard. Let your children find pictures of each seed as a plant in a garden magazine or seed catalog. Cut out the pictures and glue them next to the appropriate seeds. Do the biggest seeds always make the biggest plants?

Plants

Planting a Seed

Sung to: "The Farmer in the Dell"

The farmer plants the seeds,
The farmer plants the seeds.
Hi, ho, and cheery-oh,
The farmer plants the seeds.

Additional verses: The rain begins to fall;
The sun begins to shine; The plants begin
to grow.

Nancy H. Giles

Up Grows the Plant

Sung to: "The Mulberry Bush"

First you plant the seed in the ground.
Then you sprinkle it with water.
Next the sun shines down from above,
And up pops a plant!

Diane Thom

Little Seed

Sung to: "Twinkle, Twinkle, Little Star"

I'm a little planted seed.
Cool, sweet rain falls down on me.
Sun shines down so warm and good,
And the soil gives me my food.
I'm a little planted seed.
I have all the things I need.

Adele Engelbracht

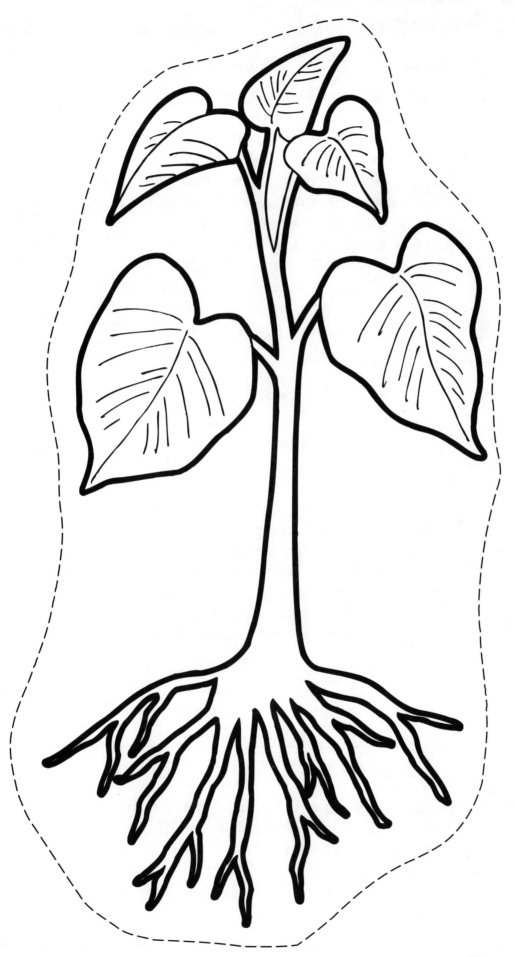

Flowers

Window Flowers

Set out crayons with the papers removed, a cheese grater, and pieces of waxed paper. Help one of your children grate some of the crayons onto one of the pieces of waxed paper. Lay another piece of waxed paper on top of the shavings. Place the pieces of waxed paper between a folded damp cloth and carefully move an iron across the cloth to melt the crayons. (Close supervision is necessary when any appliance is used by or near children.) Repeat with each child. Encourage the children to notice how the crayon colors spread and mix together. Cut the children's papers into flower shapes and hang them in a window to let the light shine through.

Lovely Lilacs

Show your children some real lilacs. Let them touch and smell the fragrant flowers. Then have them make their own lilac art. Set out precut 2-inch squares of lavender, purple, or white tissue paper. Show the children how to twist one of the paper squares around a chopstick or the eraser end of a pencil to make a lilac blossom. Let the children make as many blossoms as they wish. After each child has made several blossoms, show the children how to glue their blossoms to craft sticks to make lilac branches. Use the lilac branches as springtime centerpieces, if desired.

Hint: It takes only a dab of glue to secure the blossoms to the craft sticks. Have your children apply the glue with cotton swabs for better control.

Egg Cup Bluebells

Cut the egg cups out of cardboard egg cartons. Then cut the cups into bluebell shapes as shown in the illustration. Let the children paint the bluebell shapes blue. When the paint has dried, make stems by inserting the ends of green pipe cleaners through the bottoms of the bluebells. Bend the pipe cleaners into cane shapes and let the children thread them on their bluebell stems.

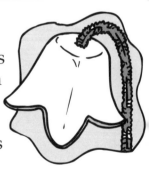

Such Pretty Flowers

Making the Flowers—Give each of your children a plain white paper plate. Divide the children into five groups. Have one group color its paper plate "flowers" red, one group yellow, one group orange, one group blue, and one group pink. Give the children green construction paper stems and leaves to attach to their plates to complete their flowers.

Reading the Poem—Have your children hold their flowers and sit in a circle. As you begin reading the poem below, have the children hunch over their flowers and pretend to be buds that have not opened yet. As you name each color of flower, have the children holding flowers of the same color uncurl themselves and stand up.

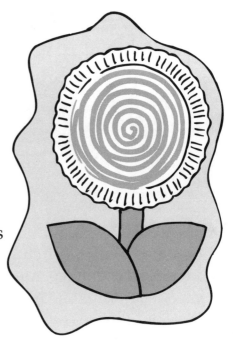

We are all such pretty flowers
Growing in Mary's garden bed.
When the rain comes down,
Up come the flowers of red.

(Red flowers stand up.)

We are flowers that have grown
In the warmth of the sun.
Mary tends us gently—
Up come the yellow ones.

(Yellow flowers stand up.)

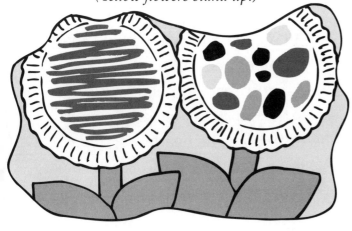

We are flowers in the springtime,
We wear our petals bright.
Up come the orange flowers,
They are quite a pretty sight.

(Orange flowers stand up.)

We are blossoms all in bloom,
Here are some in shades of blue.

(Blue flowers stand up.)

And some of us are wearing pink
That glistens in the morning dew.

(Pink flowers stand up.)

We are flowers in the garden.
We are Mary's pride and joy.
But if you look more closely,
You'll see we're girls and boys!

Susan M. Paprocki

Flowers

Flower Shop

Let your children take turns being florists and customers in your own Flower Shop. Provide a variety of artificial flowers, baskets, vases, and florist foam. Give them paper and markers to make signs for their shop. Put up pictures of flowers. Encourage them to name and describe the flowers as they are arranging them and purchasing them.

A Dandelion

Go outside with your children and help them find dandelions that have gone to seed. Let each child pick one and hold it still while you read the poem below out loud. When you get to the end of the third line, have your children blow on their dandelions.

I have a dandelion today
Whose golden hair has turned to gray,
And when I blow on it like so
    (Blow.)
Way up in the air its hair will go.

Lois E. Putnam

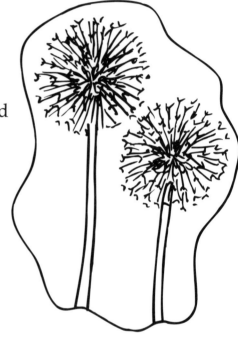

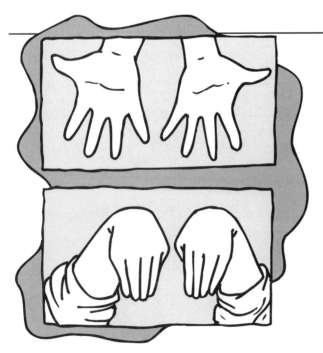

My Flower Bed

Read the poem below to your children while they act out the motions indicated.

See the purple and white blossoms
In the flower bed.
The daisy spreads it petals wide,
    (Hold palms outward with fingers open.)
The tulip bows its head.
    (Bend hands at wrist with fingers closed.)

Adapted Traditional

Guessing Garden

Cut flower shapes from several colors of paper or felt (use the flower pattern on page 168 as a guide, if you wish.) Invite your children to sit in a circle. Lay the flower shapes in the circle where everyone can see. Ask all the children to close their eyes. Let one child "pick" a flower from the garden and hide it. When the others open their eyes, see who can guess which color of flower was picked.

Flower Pot Game

Make 10 copies of the flower pot pattern on page 169. Number the copies from 1 to 10 and draw the matching number of stems coming out of each pot. Set out the flower pot pages and a box of buttons. Let your children take turns selecting one of the pages, identifying the number on it, counting out the appropriate number of buttons, and putting them on the top of the stems for flowers.

Flowers

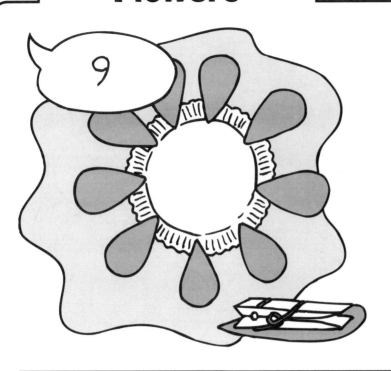

Counting Petals

Cut out ten 3½-inch-long flower petals from construction paper. Glue each petal onto a separate clothespin. Use a small paper plate as the flower center and let your children take turns clipping on the number of petals that you ask for.

Extension: Introduce beginning addition and subtraction by having your children add and remove petals from the plate.

Flower Walk

Cut out flower shapes from assorted colors of construction paper (use the flower pattern on page 168 as a guide). Arrange the flower shapes in a large circle on the floor. Have your children walk around the circle, stepping from flower to flower, as you recite the rhyme below.

Round and round the circle,
Hop, hop, hop.
Only step on flowers till
I say "Stop!"

Heather Tekavec

At the word *stop*, have your children stand on the nearest flower. Ask them to identify the color of their flower, then play the game again.

Little Flower Seeds

Ask your children to pretend to be little seeds, curled up tight in the ground. Slowly, have the children uncurl their bodies and stand up straight like seedlings. Tell them to imagine that the warm sun is shining overhead. Encourage them to reach, like little plants, toward the light, palms together in tight little buds, stretching as high as they can. Then have their buds open up into beautiful flowers soaking up the sun and swaying gently in the spring breeze.

Flower Masks

Let your children help you cut simple 3-inch flower petal shapes out of brightly colored construction paper. For each child, cut out the center of a paper plate. To make the masks, have your children turn the paper plates upside down and tape the petals around the edge. Attach craft stick handles to the bottom of the plates. Have your children put their faces through the openings in their masks and pretend to be flowers growing in the warm sunshine.

Flowers

Flowers Everywhere
Sung to: "London Bridge"

Flowers blooming here and there,
Here and there, here and there.
See the pink ones here and there,
Everywhere.

Continue with additional verses,
substituting other flower colors for *pink*.

Gayle Bittinger

Flowers Are Blooming
Sung to: "Frère Jacques"

Flowers are blooming,
Flowers are blooming,
All around, all around.
All the pretty colors,
All the pretty colors,
Dot the ground,
Dot the ground.

Let's go see them,
Let's go see them,
Blooming bright,
Blooming bright.
Use your nose to smell them.
Use your eyes to see them.
What a sight!
What a sight!

Sharon Clendenen

The World Is Filled With Color

Sung to: "Go In and Out the Window"

The flowers are blooming brightly,
The flowers are blooming brightly,
The flowers are blooming brightly,
The world is filled with color.

Jean Warren

Did You Ever See a Flower?

Sung to: "Did You Ever See a Lassie?"

Did you ever see a flower, a flower,
  a flower?
Did you ever see a flower so pretty
  and tall?
It's swaying and blowing,
In the wind, it is growing.
Did you ever see a flower so pretty and tall?

Have your children pretend to be flowers,
growing tall and swaying in the wind.

Bev Qualheim

Smell a Violet

Sung to: "Row, Row, Row Your Boat"

Smell, smell, smell a daisy,
Smell a pretty rose,
Smell a pretty violet
Tickling my nose.
Achoo!

Margo S. Miller

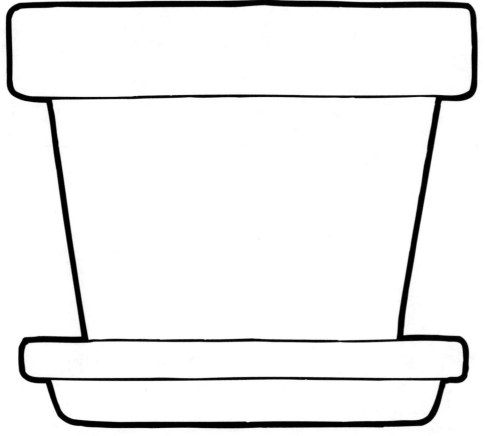

Trees

A Tree for All Seasons

A deciduous tree looks different in each of the four seasons. Help your children understand this by having them make four trees, one for each season. For each child, you will need one short cardboard tube and two plain, white paper plates. Cut two slits, directly opposite each other, in one end of each of the cardboard tubes. Cut the paper plates in half. Have your children paint their cardboard tubes brown. Then have each child use crayons or markers to decorate one paper plate half with pink blossoms, one with green leaves, one with red and orange leaves, and one with bare branches. When the children have finished, let them choose what season they want to show on their tree. Help them insert the appropriate plate into the slits in their tubes to make a tree for that season. Talk about the season. Repeat with the other seasons.

Apple Trees

Cut simple apple tree shapes out of green construction paper. Set out corks and red tempera paint. Let your children press the corks in the red tempera paint and then onto their tree shapes to make red "apples." Later, use the prints for counting practice.

Paper Collages

Discuss with your children how paper is made from trees. Talk about all the different kinds of paper they use. Let each child color a picture of a tree in the center of a piece of construction paper. Then set out different kinds of paper for them to tear into pieces and glue around their trees in collage form.

Leaf Impressions

Have your children collect a variety of tree leaves. Give each of them a small lump of modeling dough or clay. Have the children make their dough flat and smooth. Let them press the leaves into the dough. Then help them carefully remove the leaves from the dough to see the impressions left behind. Ask the children to match the impressions to the actual leaves.

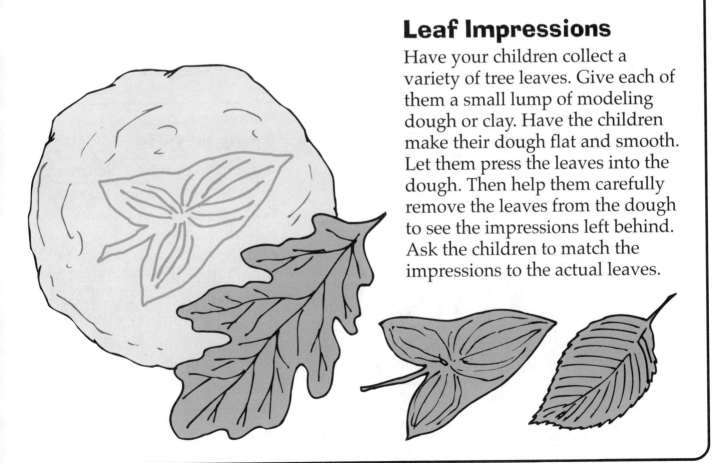

Trees

Tree Friends

Read the rhyme below out loud. Have your children act out the motions. Encourage them to think of ways they can be friends to trees.

Deep in the woods
With trees so tall,

(Stretch arms high.)

I feel so little,
So very small.

(Make self small.)

I love to look up
And see the trees bend.

(Look upward.)

I know they're saying,
"Let's all be friends."

(Hug self.)

Jean Warren

Tree Words

Attach several tree pictures to a piece of posterboard. Try to select a variety of trees in different seasons. Show your children your tree poster. Let them tell you words that describe the trees they see. Write down the children's words on the posterboard. Read the words back to your children.

Leaf Sorting

Collect a variety of fall leaves. Show the leaves to your children. Point out the different shapes and colors of the leaves. Let the children take turns sorting the leaves by shape or by color.

Leaf Matching

Collect five medium-sized leaves. Trace each of their outlines on a separate sheet of paper. Challenge your children to match each leaf to its outline.

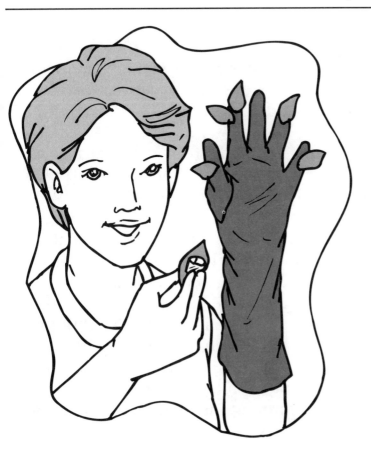

Counting Tree Leaves

Use a marker to color a long, white glove brown. Cut small leaf shapes out of felt in autumn colors. Attach loops of tape rolled sticky side out to the back of the shapes. Slip on the glove to turn your arm and hand into a "tree," and let your children attach the leaves to the finger "branches." Each time you remove the leaves, have your children count them together.

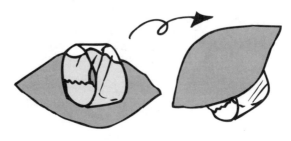

Trees

Parts of a Tree

Cut out a brown felt tree shape that includes a tree trunk and branches (use the pattern on page 178, if you wish). Cut leaf shapes out of green felt and several different kinds of fruit and nut shapes, such as apples, pears, walnuts, and almonds, out of felt scraps. (Use the patterns on page 179, if you wish.) Place the tree shape on a flannelboard. Point out the different parts of the tree. Then show the children the felt shapes. Talk about the different kinds of fruits and nuts that grow on trees. Then let the children take turns putting the leaf, fruit, and nut shapes on the felt tree.

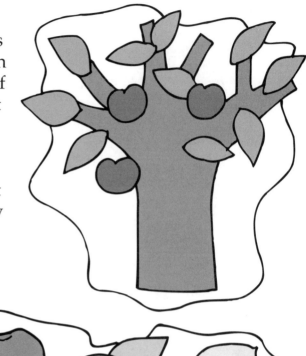

Made From Trees

Set out objects that are made from wood, such as a newspaper, a book, a toothpick, a pencil, and a block. Set out other objects that are not made from wood, such as a plastic toy car, a cotton towel, a crayon, a metal spoon, and a mirror. Explain to your children that many of the objects we use every day are made from trees. Show them the objects you collected. Let them help you sort the items into two piles. Ask them if they can think of other things that are made from trees. Have your children go on a tree hunt around the room to search for other objects that are made from trees.

Adopt-a-Tree

Have your children choose a nearby tree to adopt. Visit the tree regularly and try to incorporate it into activities throughout the year, such as the following:

* Play circle games, such as Ring Around the Rosie or Duck, Duck, Goose, around the tree.

* Make leaf and bark rubbings.

* Pick up litter around the tree.

* Talk into a tape recorder and describe what the tree looks like in a particular season.

* Observe the animals that live in or near the tree.

Plant a Little Tree

Let your children plant tree seedlings. Give each child a plastic cup and a seedling. Have the children plant their seedlings in their cups with some dirt. Explain to the children that when the trees get bigger and stronger in a few months, they can be planted outside. Then sing the song below with your children.

Hint: Information about tree seedlings and educational kits are available from The National Arbor Day Foundation. For information, write to The National Arbor Day Foundation, 100 Arbor Avenue, Nebraska City, NE 68410.

Sung to: "Pick a Bale of Cotton"

Gotta jump down, turn around,

Plant a little tree now.

Jump down, turn around,

Plant a little green.

Gotta jump down, turn around,

Plant a little tree now.

Jump down, turn around,

Plant a little green.

Martha Thomas

Trees

Tree Charades

On index cards, draw simple pictures of things you can do in a tree (climb, pick apples, etc.), things you can do under a tree (rake leaves, pick up pine cones, etc.), and things you can do to a tree (decorate it, chop it up for firewood, etc.). Have one of your children select a card and show it to the others. Then have all the children act out together the activity pictured on the card. Repeat until each child has had a chance to choose a card.

Tree Snacks

Talk about foods that grow on trees, such as apples and oranges, walnuts and almonds, olives, and chocolate (made from the seeds of the cacao tree). Let your children help you prepare some of these foods for snacktime. Give them plates and let them choose several different "tree snacks" to taste.

The Trees Are Growing

Sung to: "The Farmer in the Dell"

The trees are growing tall,
>   *(Raise arms above head, fingers touching.)*

The trees are growing tall.
With soil and rain and sunny days,
The trees are growing tall.

The trees are growing roots,
>   *(Bend over and touch floor.)*

The trees are growing roots.
With soil and rain and sunny days,
The trees are growing roots.

The trees are growing bark,
>   *(Run hands up and down sides.)*

The trees are growing bark.
With soil and rain and sunny days,
The trees are growing bark.

The trees are growing branches,
>   *(Stretch arms out.)*

The trees are growing branches.
With soil and rain and sunny days,
The trees are growing branches.

The trees are growing leaves,
>   *(Wiggle fingers.)*

The trees are growing leaves.
With soil and rain and sunny days,
The trees are growing leaves.

Susan Peters

Trees, Trees

Sung to: "Row, Row, Row Your Boat"

Trees, trees in the woods,
Growing oh, so tall.
Some have needles,
Some have leaves.
We just love them all!

Elizabeth McKinnon

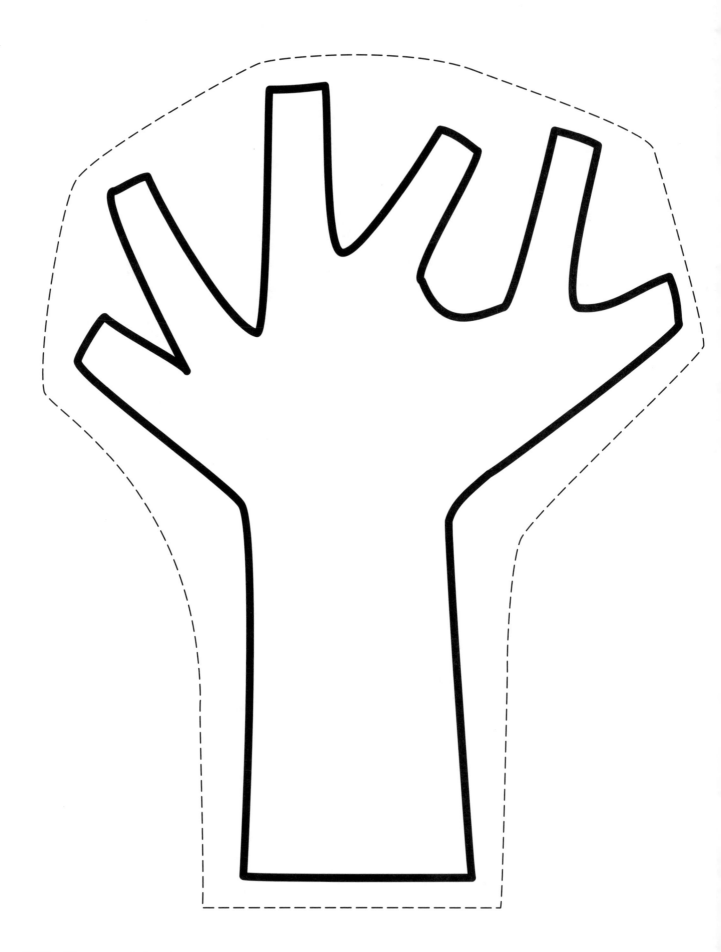

Fruits & Vegetables

Collages

Cut pictures of fruits and vegetables out of seed catalogs and garden magazines. Give your children sheets of construction paper. Let them select the pictures they like and glue them to their papers. Hang their completed collages on a wall or a bulletin board. Talk about all the different fruits and vegetables that are shown.

Fruit Shapes

Purchase an air-dry modeling compound or make your own air-dry dough (see recipe below). Set out the dough and a variety of fruits. Ask your children to look carefully at all the different shapes the fruits have. Let them use the dough to make their own fruit shapes. When the shapes are dry, let the children paint them.

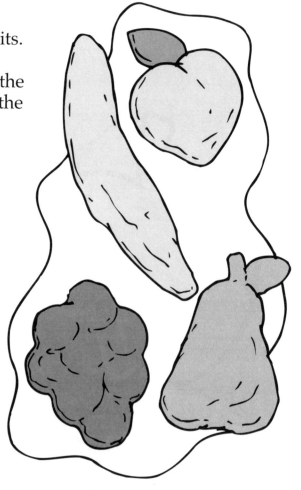

Air-Dry Dough

In a saucepan, combine 1 cup cornstarch and 2 cups baking soda. Stir in 1¼ cups water. Stirring constantly, cook over medium heat until the consistency of mashed potatoes, about 4 minutes. Remove the pan from the heat and cover it with a damp towel. Allow the dough to cool. Store dough in an airtight container.

Creating a Cornucopia

Have your children bring in fresh fruits or vegetables that they like or would like to try. Display them in a simple basket. Talk to the children about the fruits and vegetables. Encourage the children to describe the different colors, patterns, sizes, and weights. Ask questions such as these: "Which one is the biggest? Which is the smallest? How many are green? How many are yellow?"

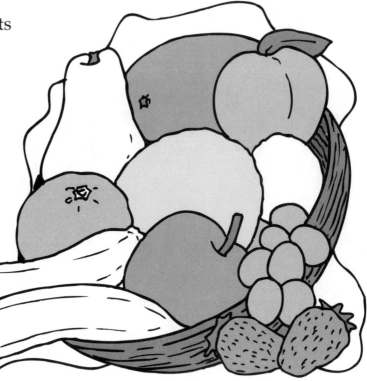

It is long and has a green top.

Which One?

Show your children the fruits and vegetables from the Creating a Cornucopia activity described above. Ask the children to listen carefully as you describe one of them. Then ask them to try to guess what it is. For example, you could say, "I'm thinking of a vegetable (or fruit) that is orange. It is long, and it has a green top. What is it?" (carrot) Give as many clues as necessary.

Extension: Let your children take turns describing fruits and vegetables for the others to guess.

Veggie Puppets

To make a Veggie Puppet, hold a vegetable by the bottom and use straight pins to pin a scrap of cloth around the vegetable so that your hand is hidden. Carve or draw on facial features, or pin on facial features cut from felt or construction paper. Almost any firm vegetable has great puppet potential. Try potatoes, zucchini, or carrots. These puppets are a fun way to discuss good eating habits with your children.

Variation: Use firm fruits, such as apples, oranges, or bananas, instead of vegetables.

Color Fruits

Using the patterns on pages 188 and 189 as guides, cut the following shapes out of felt: one yellow banana, two orange oranges, three red apples, four purple plums, and five yellow pears. Read the rhyme below out loud. As you mention each fruit, place the felt fruit shapes on a flannelboard. At the end of the rhyme, let your children help you place all the fruit shapes in a lunch bag or box.

One yellow banana extra nice,
Pretty please, give me a slice.
Two round oranges really sweet,
What a super-duper treat!
Three red apples very bright,
Hurry up and take a bite.
Four purple plums in a sack,
Make a really special snack.
Five ripe pears so great to munch.
Here, put a few in your lunch.

Lois E. Putnam

Veggie Science

Collect a variety of vegetables and set them out on a table. Place a scale, measuring tapes, a magnifying glass, and paper and pencil on the table as well. Guide your children as they do the experiments below.

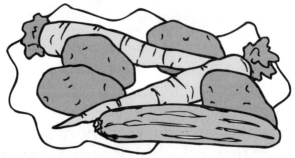

Weighing—Set out a scale and let your children weigh several of the vegetables. Which one weighs the most? Which one weighs the least?

Estimating—Put out two large potatoes and two small zucchini. Have your children estimate which pair weighs the most. Let them weigh them on a scale to check their estimates.

Predicting—Set out a pile of carrots. Have your children predict how many carrots it will take to make a pound. Have one child watch the scale as it moves up. Ask the other children to count with you as you put the carrots on the scale, one at a time. How close was their prediction?

Measuring—Let your children measure the vegetables. Talk about length (up and down), width (side to side), and diameter (around). Show them how to measure each one.

Observing—Give your children time to carefully examine each vegetable. Have them take turns using the magnifying glass. Encourage them to talk about the colors, shapes, and textures they see.

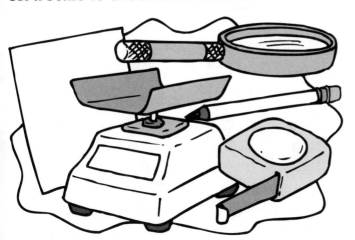

Orange Senses

Talk about the five senses with your children. Show them an orange. Have them use their sense of sight to look at it. What color is it? What shape? Do you see anything else? Pass the orange around. Let the children use their sense of touch to feel the orange. How does it feel? Have your children close their eyes and listen carefully while you peel it. Can they hear the skin being pulled off gently? Break the orange into sections. Give each child an orange section. Have them smell their orange section before tasting it.

Fruits & Vegetables

Taste Test

Cut apples and raw potatoes into small bite-size pieces. Give each of your children a plate with a piece of apple and a piece of potato on it. Have them hold their noses and take a bite of both pieces. Can they tell which is which? Our sense of taste relies very much on our sense of smell. When you can't smell, it's hard to taste the difference in foods with the same texture.

How Many Seeds?

Show your children an apple and ask them to estimate the number of seeds that will be found inside. Cut the apple open and count the seeds with the children. Have them compare the number of seeds with their estimations. Try the experiment with another apple. Does it have the same number of seeds as the first one? Try the same experiment using a different-colored apple.

Variation: Ask your children to guess how many sections are in an unpeeled orange. Then peel the orange and count the sections.

Hint: Use the fruit from this activity to make the Fruit Salad described on page 185.

How many seeds are in the apple?

Corn on the Cob

Discuss how corn grows with your children. Show them a cornstalk growing or a picture of one. Point out the ears of corn on the stalk. Purchase several ears of fresh corn for your children. Let them help husk the corn and pull off the silk. (To remove stubborn silk strands, have the children rub the ears with dry paper towels.) When they have finished, break the ears into short pieces and cook them in boiling water for 4 to 10 minutes or until tender. Cool before serving.

Making Fruit Salad

Let your children help prepare a fruit salad. Set out fruits such as bananas, oranges, apples, strawberries, and peaches. Have the children wash the fruit and help with the peeling. Let them use table knives to cut the fruit into bite-size pieces. Then have them help mix the pieces together in a large bowl. Serve the fruit salad as is or top with vanilla yogurt and granola for a special treat.

Fruit Treats

Sung to: "Frère Jacques"

I'm a grape, I'm a grape,
Growing on a vine,
Growing on a vine.
If you want some grape juice,
If you want some grape juice,
Smoosh me fine,
Smoosh me fine.

I'm a strawberry,
I'm a strawberry,
Growing on the ground,
Growing on the ground.
If you want some jam,
If you want some jam,
Mash me around,
Mash me around.

I'm an orange,
I'm an orange,
Growing on a tree,
Growing on a tree.
If you want some orange juice,
If you want some orange juice,
Just squeeze me,
Just squeeze me.

Polly Reedy

Eat, eat, eat the carrots,
And that is what they did.

Planting

Sung to: "Bingo"

There were some kids who wanted carrots
And this is what they did:
Plant, plant, plant the carrots,
Plant, plant, plant the carrots,
Plant, plant, plant the carrots,
And that is what they did.

Additional verses: Water the carrots; Weed the carrots; Pick the carrots; Cook the carrots; Eat the carrots.

Let your children decide what vegetable they would like to sing about. Substitute the name of that vegetable for *carrot*.

Nancy Nason Biddinger

Vegetables

Sung to: "Twinkle, Twinkle, Little Star"

Vegetables, vegetables, use a hoe,
Vegetables, vegetables, soon will grow.
Vegetables, vegetables, corn and potatoes,
Vegetables, vegetables, squash and tomatoes.
Vegetables, vegetables, washed and clean,
Vegetables, vegetables, red and green.

Vegetables, vegetables, what a treat,
Vegetables, vegetables, can't be beat.
Vegetables, vegetables, on a tray,
Vegetables, vegetables, every day.
Vegetables, vegetables, such good food,
Vegetables, vegetables, baked or stewed.

Vegetables, vegetables, on my plate,
Vegetables, vegetables, taste just great.
Vegetables, vegetables, are good for you.
Vegetables, vegetables, have a few.
Vegetables, vegetables, carrots and peas,
Vegetables, vegetables, have more, please.

Barbara B. Fleisher

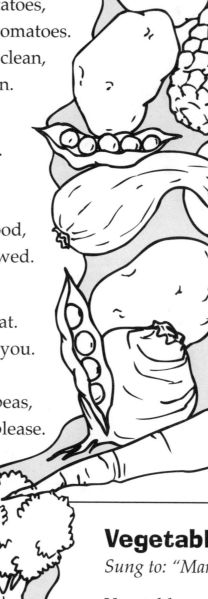

Vegetables Are Plants

Sung to: "Mary Had a Little Lamb"

Vegetables are plants we eat,
They're so good, what a treat!
Carrots, beans, and broccoli,
They help us grow so healthily.

Gayle Bittinger

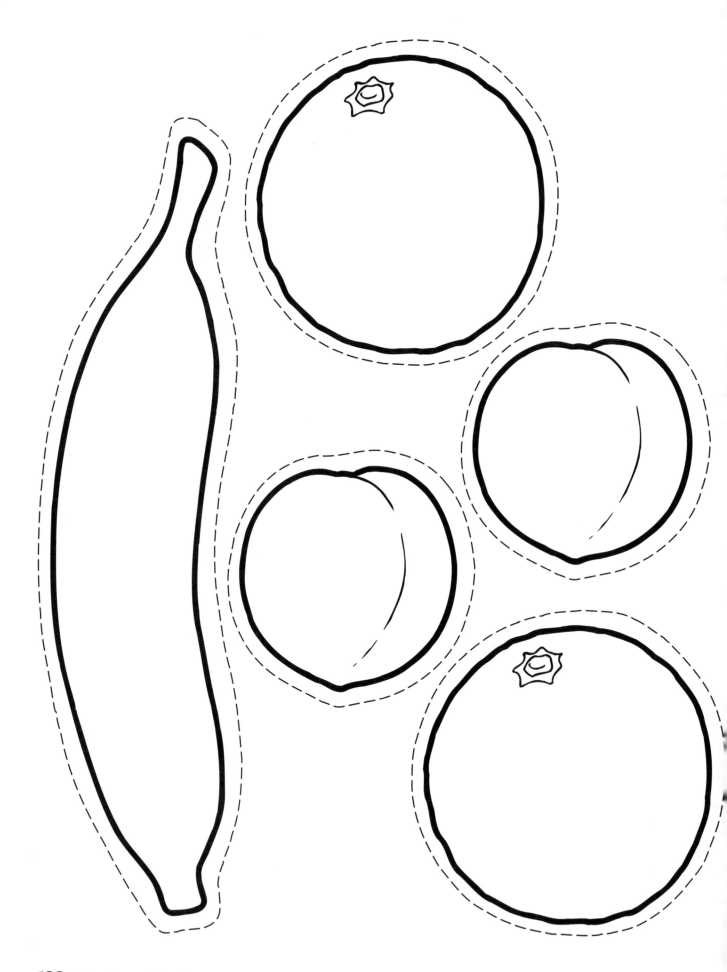

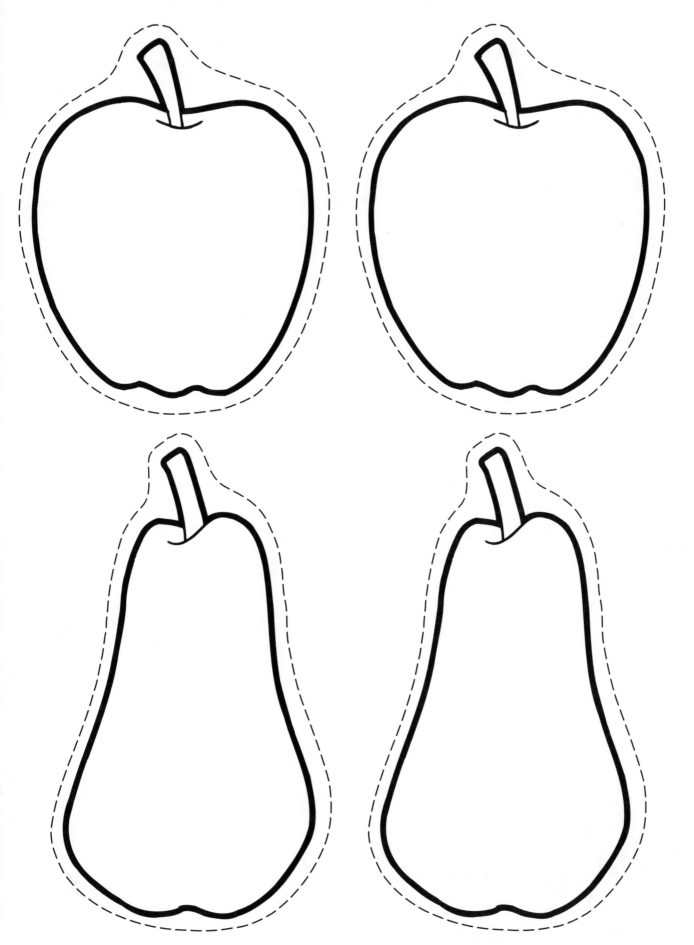

Weather

Wind

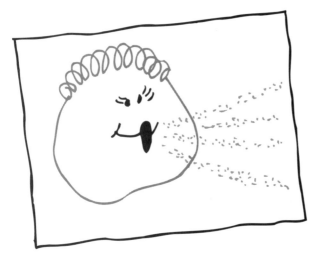

Mrs. Wind

Give each of your children a piece of construction paper. Have the children use crayons to draw pictures on their papers of what they think Mrs. Wind looks like. Then have each child use a small brush to paint glue coming out of Mrs. Wind's mouth. Help the child sprinkle glitter, sand, or salt onto the glue and shake off the excess.

Wind Catchers

For each of your children, collect a cardboard milk carton. Cut off the bottom of each carton and cut a "door" in each side. (Make sure the doors open in the same direction.) Fold the doors of each carton open and let your children paint the cartons with a mixture of powdered tempera paint and liquid soap. Punch a hole in the top of each carton and tie a piece of string through it. Hang the finished Wind Catchers outside and watch them twirl.

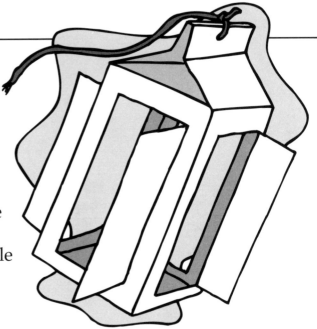

Bag Kites

Have your children make beautiful kites to fly on a windy day. Provide each child with a small paper bag. Let the children decorate their bags with crayons or markers. Punch a hole on the top side of each bag near the opening and tie a piece of yarn through the hole. (You may wish to reinforce the hole with tape.) Show your children how the kites will fill with air and fly up and down when the children run with them.

Windy Art

Take your children outside on a windy day. Give each child a piece of construction paper with a few drops of tempera paint on it. Have the children hold their papers up and let the wind blow the paint into designs.

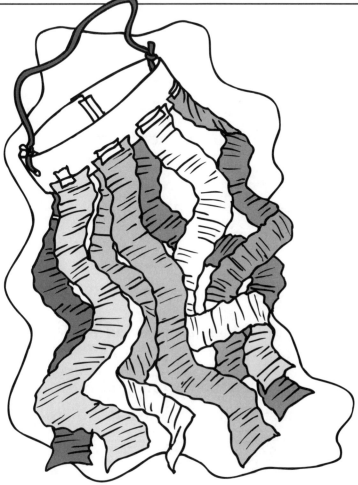

Windsocks

Cut cardboard into 1-by-18-inch strips. Bend each strip into a circle and securely tape or staple it in place. Cut crepe paper into strips about 2 feet long. Give each of your children one of the cardboard circles. Let the children tape the crepe paper strips around their circles so the strips all hang down. To complete each Windsock, punch two holes in the cardboard circle opposite each other and tie a 3-foot piece of yarn through them. Hang the Windsocks in a windy area and let the children watch the wind make their crepe paper strips dance and sway. Or, let the children run outside with their Windsocks floating behind them.

Wind

Feel the Wind

Read the poem below to your children. Ask them to think of other ways they can feel the wind blowing.

Feel the wind
As you walk along
Blowing, blowing,
Wild and strong.

Feel the wind
Whip up the air,
Knock off your hat,
Mess up your hair.

Feel the wind
Nip at your nose,
Race round your feet,
Tug on your clothes.

Feel the wind
As you walk along
Blowing, blowing
Wild and strong.

Lois E. Putnam

When the Hats Blow

Using the patterns on page 197, cut simple hat shapes out of the following colors of felt: blue, yellow, red, brown, green, black, orange, white, and purple. As you read the poem below, "fly" each hat, as it is named, to your flannelboard.

When I hear the winds blow,
I look up in the sky.
Instead of things like birds or planes,
I watch the hats fly by.

Each one different from the last,
Every color do I see.
Some are big and some are small,
As they fly by me.

Here comes a blue hat flying by,
Now a yellow hat in the sky.
Next a red hat on its way,
Then a brown hat flies away.

Green and black, orange and white,
Even purple, what a sight!
I like it when there's rain and snow,
But most of all when the hats blow.

Jean Warren

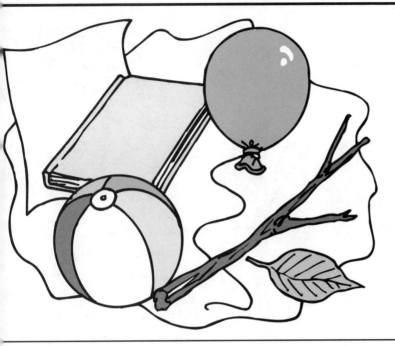

Wind Experiment

On a windy day, let your children go outside and experiment with the wind. Take out several pairs of objects, such as a piece of paper and a book, a leaf and a tree branch, and a balloon and a ball. Ask the children why the wind moves some of the things but not the others. Let the children observe the weight of the objects compared to the strength of the wind.

Wind Watching

Hang some ready-made windsocks and wind chimes outside where your children can see them. Let the children watch the windsocks and chimes swing and sway when the wind blows. Can they tell in which direction the wind is moving? How hard is the wind blowing?

Windy Scarves

Let each of your children experiment with a scarf. Play some music while your children whirl and twirl with their scarves. Then tell the children that the scarves represent the wind. Have them use their scarves to show you gentle breezes, sudden gusts, gale winds, and tornadoes.

Wind

Moving Air
Sung to: "Old MacDonald"

Wind is when the air is moving,
Going here and there.
It waves the flags and shakes the trees,
And messes up my hair.
With a puff-puff here and a puff-puff there,
Here a puff, there a puff, everywhere a puff-puff.
Wind is when the air is moving,
Going here and there.

Sometimes wind is moving slow,
Sometimes very fast.
Sometimes with a gentle poof,
Sometimes with a blast.
With a puff-puff here and a puff-puff there,
Here a puff, there a puff, everywhere a puff-puff.
Sometimes wind is moving slow,
Sometimes very fast.

Margo S. Miller

Blow the Wind
Sung to: "Row, Row, Row Your Boat"

Blow, blow, blow the wind
Gently through the trees.
Blow, and blow, and blow, and blow.
How I like a breeze!

Blow, blow, blow the clouds,
Blow them through the sky.
Blow, and blow, and blow, and blow.
Watch the clouds roll by!

Diane Thom

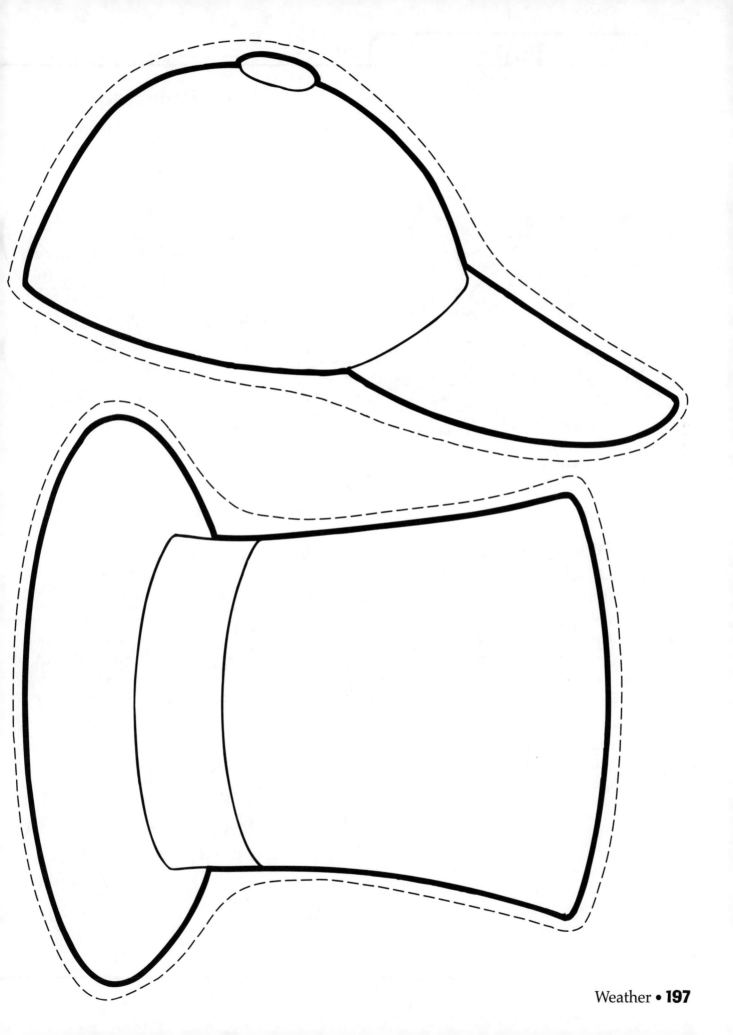

Rain

Rain Painting

On a rainy day, give each of your children a paper plate. Let the children sprinkle a few drops of food coloring on their plates. Have them put on their raincoats and walk outside, holding their plates in the rain for a few moments. After they bring their plates inside, talk about the designs created by the rain.

Raindrop Collage

Let your children look through magazines to find pictures of rain. Have them tear or cut out the pictures. Cut a large raindrop shape out of butcher paper. Let the children glue the pictures on the raindrop shape to make a Raindrop Collage. Encourage them to talk about the rain in each picture. Can they see any raindrops?

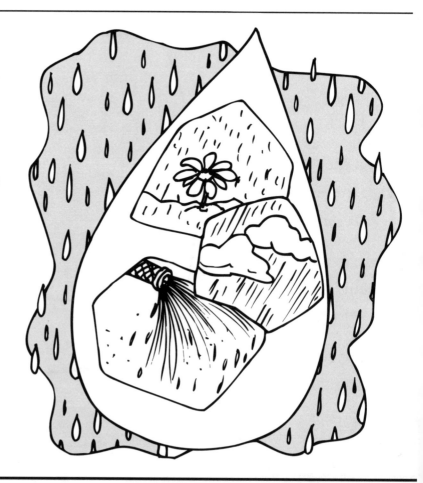

Rainy Day Rhythm

Begin by saying, "I hear a storm coming." Then say the rhyme below and have your children act out the motions described in the rhyme. When you get to the fifth verse, begin tapping children on the shoulder to have them stop "raining."

I hear thunder, I hear rain.

(Cup hand behind ear.)

Can you help me make the same?

Raindrops falling, falling down.
Can you help me make their sound?

(Slap hands on floor or table.)

Softly first, the raindrops fall.

(Slap hands softly.)

Now make your fingers form a ball.

(Make fists and pound them on floor or table.)

Faster, faster, the raindrops come.

(Pound fists faster.)

Sounds like pounding on a drum.

What a racket, what a sound,
I wish this storm would please calm down.

(Begin tapping children on the shoulder.)

At last, at last, the raindrops stop,
The rain is stopping, drop by drop.

(Make pounding quieter and quieter.)

Now the storm is gone at last.
I'm just glad this storm is past.

Patty Claycomb

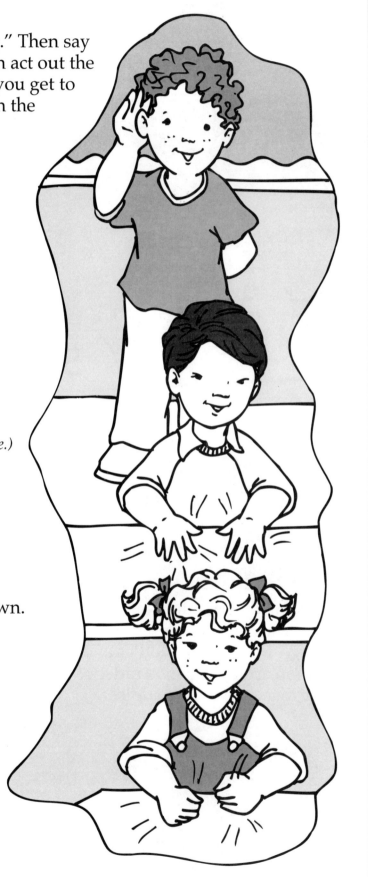

Rain

Counting Raindrops

Make five copies of the rain cloud patterns on page 203. Cut out the shapes, number them from 1 to 10, and cover them with clear self-stick paper. Set out the cloud shapes and a black crayon. Let your children take turns identifying the number on each cloud and drawing on the matching number of raindrops. Wipe the clouds with a dry cloth to erase the crayon marks for the next child.

Hint: Use more or less clouds, depending on the abilities of your children. Add a matching number of small dots to each cloud for children just learning to identify numerals.

Rain Puddles

Cut rain puddles out of brown construction paper. Vary the puddles in size from small to large. Mix up the puddles and let your children arrange them in order of size. Help them count the puddles.

Rain Senses

Watch the rain with your children. Is it raining a little or a lot? Have the children put on rain clothes and go outside. Can they see the raindrops falling on the ground? On the trees? What sounds does the rain make? What does the rain feel like on their faces? Does the air smell different when it rains? Have them follow a stream of rain to a puddle or a storm drain. Where do they think the raindrops go after that?

Rain Watching

Make a rain gauge by using a permanent marker to mark inch measurements on the side of a clear-plastic jar. Place the jar outside. Each day, have your children bring the jar inside to check for rainfall. Keep track of the rainfall on a chart.

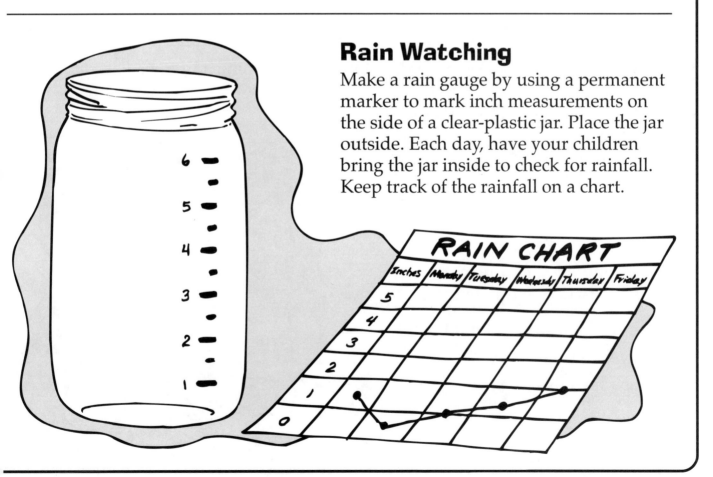

RAIN CHART

Inches	Monday	Tuesday	Wednesday	Thursday	Friday
5					
4					
3					
2					
1					
0					

Rain

Little Rain Cloud

Sung to: "I'm a Little Teapot"

I'm a little rain cloud in the sky,
I'm full of raindrops way up high.
When I'm full enough,
Here's what I'll do,
I'll spill my raindrops right on you!

Margo S. Miller

It Is Raining

Sung to: "She'll Be Comin' Round the Mountain"

It is raining, raining, raining all around,
It is raining, raining, raining all around,
Hear its drip-a-drip-a-drip-drop,
Hear its plip-a-plip-a-plip-plop,
It is raining, raining, raining all around.

Lois E. Putnam

Rainy Day

Sung to: "Twinkle, Twinkle, Little Star"

Rainy, rainy, rainy day,
Water puddles all for play.
The sky is cloudy, but I don't mind,
Puddles, galoshes, and mud pies.
Rainy, rainy, rainy day,
In the rain, I like to play.

Kristine Wagoner

Snow

Snowy Pictures

Set out a bowl of popped popcorn and several small bowls of glue. Give each of your children a piece of construction paper. Have the children dip pieces of popcorn into the glue and then press them onto their construction paper. Encourage them to make snowy designs on their papers with the popcorn.

Snowstorm Art

Look through magazines to find pictures of outdoor scenes without snow. Set out the magazine pictures, a large sturdy box, white tempera paint, a paintbrush, and an apron. Invite your children, one at a time, to join you at the box. Have the children put on the apron, select one of the pictures, and place it in the box. Show them how to dip the bristles of the paintbrush into the white paint and then shake it over the picture to create a "snowstorm." Let the children add as much or as little snow as they wish to their pictures.

Snowman for the Birds

If you have snow outside, let your children make this fun and useful snow creation. Have the children begin making snowmen as usual, but instead of using rocks and twigs to decorate them, give them birdseed and other bird treats for decorations. Some ideas include edible necklaces made from popcorn or O-shaped cereal, a hat or scarf made from pressed-on birdseed, stale bread cut into shapes with cookie cutters for buttons or clothing decorations, and a carrot nose spread with peanut butter and rolled in birdseed. Encourage your children to think of other bird-friendly ways to decorate their snow creations.

Snow Story

Read the story below out loud to your children. Let them fill in the blanks as you go along.

Snowflakes fall as softly as _____,

And as quietly as _____.

The snow is as cold as _____.

I love to watch the snow cover up _____.

I love walking in the snow like a _____.

I think I will save some snow in my _____.

The snow makes me happy because _____.

Sometimes the snow makes me sad because _____.

Jean Warren

Snow Math

Fill a large tub with snow. Bring it indoors and place it on a towel on a low table or the floor. Set out measuring cups and spoons by the tub. Let your children explore the snow with the cups and spoons. How many little cups of snow does it take to fill up the big cup? How many spoons of snow fill up the medium-sized cup? Which is more, one big cup or two little cups? Bring in new snow as the snow in the tub melts.

Hint: If you don't have snow in your area, use a tub full of cotton balls.

Snow

Melting Snow

Fill a clear-plastic cup with snow (or freeze some water in a cup). Show the cup to your children. Ask them what will happen to the snow (or ice) when you leave the cup in a warm room. Talk about the volume of snow in the cup. Volume is the amount of space something takes up. Have your children predict if there will be more or less volume in the cup when the snow melts. Use a permanent marker to draw a line at the volume of snow in the cup. Let your children check their predictions when the snow has completely melted.

Collecting Snowflakes

When it is snowing in your area, give your children black construction paper to take outside. Let them try to catch snowflakes on their papers. What do the snowflakes look like? Let them take turns using a magnifying glass to look closely at their snowflakes.

Hint: If you have no snow, let your children look at ice crystals from a freezer.

It's Snowing

Set up a wading pool indoors and fill it with several bags of white cotton balls. Let your children get in the pool two or three at a time. Show them how to scoop up the cotton balls and drop them on their heads to create a mini-snowstorm.

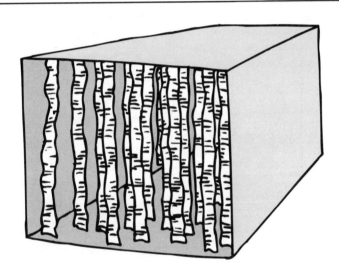

Indoor Snowstorm

Create a tunnel in your room with a large appliance box. Let your children help you hang long strips of white crepe paper in the tunnel. Have your children take turns crawling through the "snowstorm" in the tunnel.

Snow Charades

Photocopy the game cards on page 209. Mix up the cards and put them in a pile. Let one of your children select a card and show it to the group. Have the child lead everyone in acting out that snow movement.

Snow

Snowflakes

Sung to: "Twinkle, Twinkle, Little Star"

Snowflakes, snowflakes dance around,
Snowflakes, snowflakes touch the ground.
Snowflakes, snowflakes in the air,
Snowflakes, snowflakes everywhere.
Snowflakes, snowflakes dance around,
Snowflakes, snowflakes touch the ground.

Jean Warren

Build a Snowman

Sung to: "Frère Jacques"

Build a snowman,
Build a snowman,
Big and round,
Big and round.
Sun is shining on him,
Sun is shining on him.
He's all gone,
He's all gone.

Saundra Winnett

It Is Snowing

*Sung to: "Oh, Dear, What
Can the Matter Be?"*

Oh, dear, it is snowing,
Oh, dear, it is snowing,
Oh, dear, it is snowing.
What is it snowing on?

It is snowing on my nose,
It is snowing on my toes,
It is snowing on my clothes.
That's what it's snowing on.

Jean Warren

Sun

Sun Prints

Take your children outside to collect leaves, small rocks, and twigs. Have them arrange their items on pieces of dark-colored construction paper. Then help your children find a sunny spot where the wind will not blow the items away. Have them set their papers in the sunny spot. After several hours, have your children lift their items and observe the color of the paper underneath. (The sun faded all the areas that were not covered by the objects.)

Sun Art

Give each of your children a yellow construction paper circle for a sun. Set out 1-inch squares of yellow crepe paper or tissue paper. Let your children brush glue on their circles and place the paper squares on top of the glue. When the glue has dried, cut slits into the circles to make sun rays. Display the suns on a wall or a bulletin board, if desired.

Sunshine

Let your children fill in the blanks as you recite the rhyme below.
There are no right or wrong answers. Repeat the rhyme until
each child has had a chance to fill in a blank.

The morning sun peeked through the trees

To kiss the _____ and the honeybees.

It danced by the _____ and the field of hay,

Until it reached the _____, where it stayed all day.

Sun, sun, don't you run,

Stay with me and have some fun.

Shine on the _____, shine on me.

Shine on the _____, shine on the tree.

Shine on the _____, shine so fair.

Shine on the _____, shine everywhere!

Jean Warren

Shadow Friend

Share the poem below with your
children when they are outside on a
sunny day. Have them look for their
shadows as they go inside.

Sun is shining, let's go for a walk.

Hurry outside and around the block.

At your side walks a little friend, too.

Does the very same things you do.

Open the door and go inside—

Where, oh, where does my shadow
   friend hide?

Mildred Hoffman

Sun

Matching Suns

Make two copies of the game cards on page 215. Cut out the cards, color the suns yellow, and cover the cards with clear self-stick paper for durability, if you wish. Mix up the cards and show them to your children. Pick out two cards. Have your children look carefully at the cards to see if they match. If they do, put the cards aside. If they don't, put the cards back in the pile. Continue until you and your children have found all the matching suns. Then let your children take turns finding the matching suns themselves.

Disappearing Shadows

Take your children outside on a sunny day. Point out their shadows. Let them make their shadows dance and jump and move around. Then challenge them to find ways to make their shadows disappear. Can they step into the shadow of a tree so that their shadow is hidden in the larger tree's shadow? Can they find a place where the sun is not shining? Help them notice that the sun shining on them makes their shadows.

Sundial

Explain to your children that light shines down from the sun. When the light hits something solid, it makes a shadow. Tell them that the very first clocks that were made depended on the sun and the shadows it made. Then help the children make their own Sundial and keep track of the shadows made by the sun.

To begin, securely attach an empty spool to the center of a piece of cardboard. Stand a pencil in the hole of the spool. (You can support the pencil with a little modeling dough dropped into the hole.) Have your children place the Sundial outside in a place that will get sun all day. Mark the place on the cardboard where the pencil's shadow falls and note the time. Then, every 30 to 60 minutes, take one or two children outside to watch as you make a mark where the shadow is and write down the time. At the end of the day, have your children look at the marks. What kind of pattern do the marks make? Leave the sundial where it is. Let the children use it to tell time the following day.

Variation: Instead of making marks of the actual time, put a mark on the Sundial every time an activity changes. Let your children use the clock the following day to tell when it's time to play outside, time for snack, and time to go home.

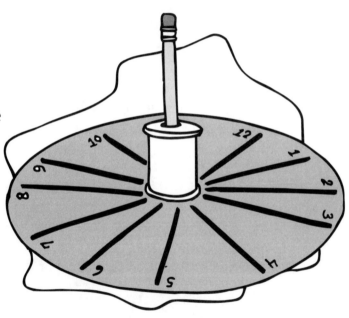

Shadow Tag

On a sunny day, go outside with your children to play Shadow Tag. Show your children how to play. Explain that, instead of touching a person to be It, you touch his or her shadow with your own shadow. Choose one child to be It and begin your game.

Sun

Sunny Day Dance

Cut a large sun shape out of yellow construction paper. Show the sun to your children. Ask them to join you in a special Sunny Day Dance. When the sun is "shining," have them dance all around. When the sun "sets," have them stop in place until it shines again.

If you wish, sing the song below, making your sun "rise" and "set" as directed.

Sung to: "The Muffin Man"

I like to dance when the sun is shining,
> *(Hold up sun shape and dance.)*

Sun is shining, sun is shining.
I like to dance when the sun is shining,
But when it sets, I stop.
> *(Put the sun shape down and stop.)*

See me twirl when the sun is shining,
> *(Hold up sun shape and dance.)*

Sun is shining, sun is shining.
See me twirl when the sun is shining,
But when it sets, I stop.
> *(Put the sun shape down and stop.)*

Additional verses: See me spin; See me leap; Hear me sing.

Gayle Bittinger

Shine So Bright

Sung to: "Three Blind Mice"

Shine so bright, shine so bright.
Big yellow sun, big yellow sun.
The sun in the sky does shine so bright,
It brings us warmth, it brings us light,
Sunshine is such a lovely sight,
Shine so bright.

Gayle Bittinger

Weather Watching

Stormy Skies

Cut raindrop, cloud, and lightning bolt shapes out of heavy paper. Let your children decorate the raindrop shapes with glitter, the cloud shapes with cotton balls, and the lightning bolt shapes with aluminum foil. Attach a piece of string to each shape and hang them from your ceiling to create Stormy Skies indoors.

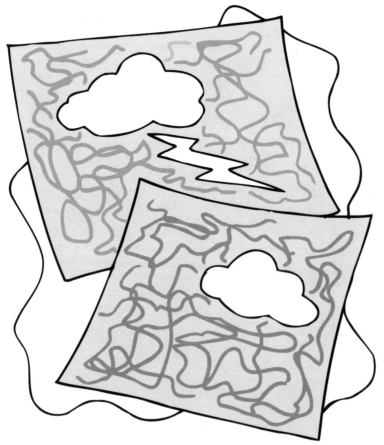

Thunderstorm Prints

Place a generous amount of black and white fingerpaint on a low table or other washable surface. (Add a little dish soap for easy cleanup.) Play a tape of storm sounds and encourage your children to fingerpaint to it. When they are finished, place cloud-shaped pieces of paper on their fingerpaintings to make Thunderstorm Prints. If you wish, when the paint dries, add a lightning bolt to each cloud.

Listening to Storms

Thunder and other sounds associated with storms can be frightening for many children. To help your children become accustomed to storm sounds, find a nature tape with storm sounds on it (many libraries have these) or tape-record your own storm. Let your children take turns listening to the tape. Show the children how to turn the volume down and up, so they can make a storm as quiet or as loud as they like.

Weather Wear

Collect an assortment of clothes for various kinds of weather such as sunny, rainy, cold, hot, etc. (The clothes should be large enough for children to slip over the clothes they are already wearing.) Have three or four children dress up in the clothes. Then have the children show their Weather Wear to the group. Ask the group to guess what kind of weather each child is dressed for.

Weather Watching

Weather Chart

Divide a long piece of butcher paper into three sections. At the top of one section, write the word "snow" and glue on some white plastic-foam packaging material for snowflakes. At the top of another section, write the word "rain" and glue on aluminum-foil raindrop shapes. At the top of the final section, write the word "sun" and glue on a large yellow sun shape. Show your children the butcher paper and talk about the weather conditions shown in the sections. Ask them to tell you words that describe each kind of weather. Write the words in the appropriate sections. Then have them look through catalogs and magazines to find pictures of items and clothing that would be used in each kind of weather. Let them tear out the pictures and glue them in the appropriate sections.

Weather Wheel

Photocopy the weather wheel and arrow patterns on page 222. Glue the weather wheel and arrow to heavy paper and cut them out. If desired, color the wheel and arrow and cover them with clear self-stick paper. Attach the arrow to the wheel by pushing a brass paper fastener through the black dot. Show the wheel to your children. Have them listen carefully while you describe one of the weather conditions shown on the wheel. Let one child come up and turn the arrow to the weather you are describing. Then let that child describe another weather condition. Continue until each child has had a turn.

Variation: Show the wheel to your children each day and let one of them point the arrow to the picture that represents the day's weather.

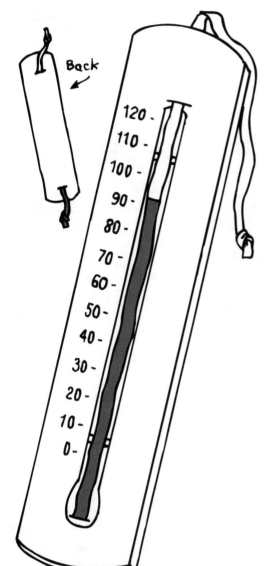

Thermometer Fun

Photocopy the thermometer pattern on page 223. Glue it to a piece of heavy paper and, if desired, color it. Cut a small slit at the top and bottom of the thermometer as indicated by the dotted lines. Color half of a 16-inch white ribbon red. Thread the ribbon through the slits and tie a knot in each end. Show your children the thermometer. Talk about how real thermometers are used to tell the temperature of the air. Show them what a thermometer looks like when it is cold (very little red ribbon showing) and what it looks like when it is hot (lots of red ribbon showing). Then play this game with your children. Adjust the ribbon on the thermometer to "hot" or "cold." Show the thermometer to the children. If it is showing cold weather, have them wrap their arms around themselves and say "Brrr." If it is showing hot weather, have them fan themselves with their hands. Let them take turns adjusting the ribbon on the thermometer.

Temperature Chart

Place a large outdoor thermometer in a spot where your children can easily see it. Have the children check the temperature on the thermometer throughout the day. Help them keep track of the temperatures on a chart. What was the coldest temperature today? What was the warmest?

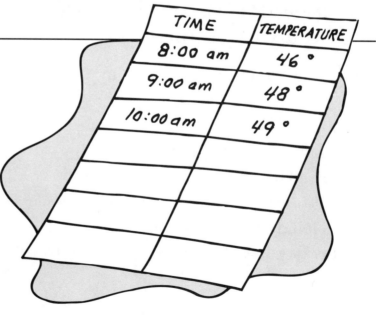

TIME	TEMPERATURE
8:00 am	46 °
9:00 am	48 °
10:00 am	49 °

Clouds in the Sky

Ask your children to tell you about clouds. What do clouds look like? What do they do? Talk about the rain and snow that clouds bring. Let your children pretend to be clouds and float around as you recite the rhyme below. Encourage them to act out the motions for each kind of cloud as they are described. Substitute the number of children in your group for *eight*.

Eight little clouds went out to play
On a bright and sunny day.
    (Float around room.)
They joined hands and circled round
    (Join hands.)
Now no sun shines on the ground.
Now the sky was cold and gray,
A cloudy day was here to stay.

Eight little clouds went out to play
On a cold and windy day.
    (Float around room.)
They filled their pockets with ice and snow
    (Pretend to fill pockets.)
Then emptied them out as they drifted below.
    (Sprinkle out snow.)
Now the world was covered with white,
A snowy day, what a sight!

Eight little clouds went out to play
On a cold and windy day.
    (Float around.)
They saw no sun up in the sky,
So they all began to cry.
    (Shake arms and fingers to represent rain falling down.)
Down fell drops from the sky,
A rainy day, my, oh, my!

Jean Warren

What's the Weather?

Sung to: "Frère Jacques"

What's the weather?
What's the weather?
Do you know?
Do you know?
Do you see the sun out?
Is there rain all about?
What's the weather?
What's the weather?

Gayle Bittinger

During a Big Storm

Sung to: "Down by the Station"

During a big storm
On a summer evening,
See all the lightning flashes
Dart to and fro.
Hear the thunder boomers
As they rumble, rumble,
"Boom, boom, boom, boom!"
Hear them go!

Lois E. Putnam

Whenever I Hear Thunder

Sung to: "Go In and Out the Window"

Whenever I hear thunder,
Up in the sky on yonder,
I never fret or wonder,
I know why it is so.

Hot air and cold are meeting,
Sound waves they are creating,
They're shouting out a greeting
To everyone below.

Margo S. Miller

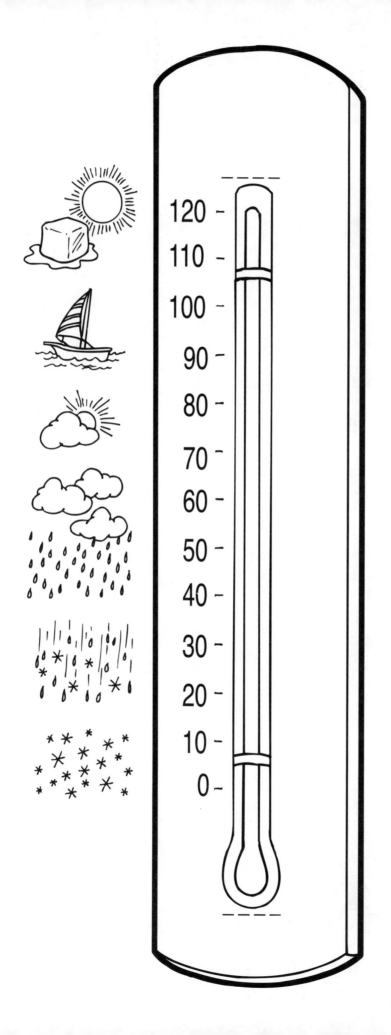

Earth and Sky

Dirt

Mud Sculpting

Set out a bucket of dirt, kitchen basters, dishpans, and a bowl of water. Let your children use their hands to put scoops of dirt in the dishpans. Have them use the kitchen basters to add water to the dirt to make mud. Let them play and be creative with the mud in their dishpans. What would happen if they added more dirt? What would happen if they added more water? Ask them to describe how the mud feels. Does it feel cold? Warm? Squishy? Slimy? Smooth? Rough?

Feet Only

Outside, fill a large tub with mud. Place several chairs around the tub. Help your children remove their shoes and socks. Let them take turns sitting in the chairs and putting their feet in the mud. Let them explore the mud with their feet. Can they cover their feet in mud? Can they dig holes with their feet? Is it easy or hard to make mud pies? Have a bucket of water and a towel close by for rinsing off and drying muddy feet.

Dirt Is Home

Photocopy the flannelboard patterns on page 231. Color and cut them out, and then glue felt strips to the back of them. Sing the rhyme below to your children. Place each shape on your flannelboard as it is mentioned in the song.

Sung to: "Alouette"

Dirt is home for many living creatures.

Dirt is home for many living things.

Look in dirt so loose or firm.

Find an insect. Find a worm.

Find a plant. Find a seed.

Rich soil is what they need.

Dirt is home for many living creatures.

Dirt is home for many living things.

Diane Thom

Mix, Mix, Mix the Mud

Let your children use their imaginations and act out the muddy movements to the song below. Real mud is not needed!

Sung to: "Row, Row, Row Your Boat"

Mix, mix, mix the mud,
Mix it with your feet.
Feel the gooey, slimy globs,
Isn't this a treat!

Mix, mix, mix the mud,
Mix it with your tummy.
Slip and slide on your side,
Don't we all look funny!

Mix, mix, mix the mud,
Mix it with your hand.
Squish it, slosh it, make mounds of it,
Doesn't this look grand!

Nancy Nason Biddinger

Dirt

Dirt Jar

Put some dirt in a jar with some water. Let your children stir up the dirt and water and notice what happens. Have them observe the jar later to see what has happened to the dirt and water. Why is most of the dirt on the bottom of the jar?

Buried Treasure

Fill several dishpans with dirt and let your children watch as you bury "treasure" such as unusual rocks or small plastic toys. Set out small shovels. Let your children dig in the dirt, searching for the Buried Treasure. When they have found everything they can, have them count their treasures.

Variation: Collect two of each treasure. Bury one set and place the other set on a tray. Have the children dig in the dirt to find one of the treasures and place it next to the matching object on the tray. Have them continue until they've found every treasure.

Dirt Safari

Take your children outside. Spread some newspaper out on the ground and put two or three scoops of dirt on it. Give your children sifters and magnifying glasses to use to examine the dirt. Can they see any parts of plants, animals, or rocks in the dirt? What does the dirt feel and smell like?

Making Dirt

Let your children help you tear fruit and vegetable skins into small pieces and crush eggshells into tiny bits. Then give them plastic cups and spoons. Have each child put in his or her cup a spoonful of sand, a spoonful of peat moss, a few pieces of fruit and vegetable skins, and some crushed eggshells. Let the children add small amounts of water to their cups before stirring all their ingredients together. They now have dirt. Give each of the children one or two bean seeds to plant in their cups. Have them set their cups in the sun and add water regularly. What are their seeds doing? What is in dirt that seeds need to grow?

Dirt

I Love Dirt

Sung to: "Three Blind Mice"

I love dirt, I love dirt.
Fun, brown, dirt; fun, brown, dirt.
I love to dig down in the ground,
I love to have dirt all around,
I love to pile it in a mound.
I love dirt.

Gayle Bittinger

Mud Song

Sung to: "Skip to My Lou"

Scoop up some dirt
And add a little water,
Scoop up some dirt
And add a little water,
Scoop up some dirt
And add a little water.
That's how I make mud.

Gayle Bittinger

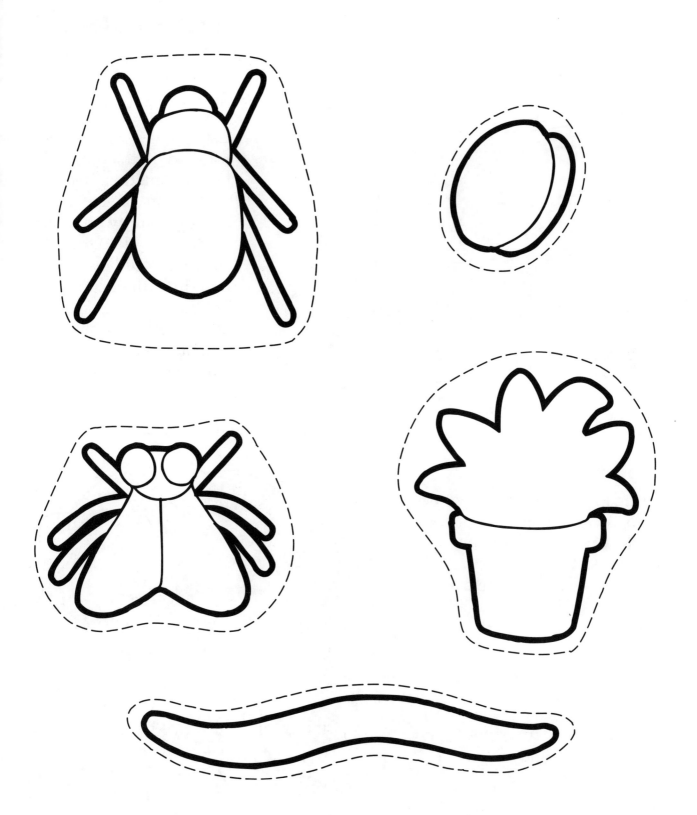

Rocks

Rock Gardens

Collect clear-plastic deli food containers and lids. You'll need one per child. Now take your children on a rock hunt. Let each child collect enough rocks to fill the bottom of his or her container. Back in your room, have your children empty out their containers. Help them squeeze liquid glue onto the bottom of their containers. Let them arrange their rocks any way they wish on the glue to make their Rock Gardens. Display the Rock Gardens in your room.

Painted Rock

Bring in the largest rock you can find or carry. Place it on some newspaper spread out on a low table. Set out tempera paint in small containers and paintbrushes. Let the children work together to paint the rock. When the paint dries, admire their creation and take a photograph of the rock and its artists. The next day, let them paint over the rock and create a new design.

Variation: If you have a large rock in your yard, consider letting children turn it into a Painted Rock.

Found a Rock

Using the patterns on page 237, cut the following shapes out of felt: a red hat, a pair of yellow socks, green pants, and a blue shoe. Sing the song below to your children. Let them take turns placing the shapes on the flannelboard as they are mentioned in the song.

Sung to: "Found a Peanut"

Found a rock, found a rock,
Found a rock in my red hat.
Just now I found a rock,
Found a rock just like that.

Found a rock, found a rock,
Found a rock in my yellow socks.
Just now I found a rock,
Found a rock for my rock box.

Found a rock, found a rock,
Found a rock in my green pants.
Just now I found a rock,
Found a rock, I think I'll dance.

Found a rock, found a rock,
Found a rock in my blue shoe.
Just now I found a rock,
Found a rock, what should I do?

Gayle Bittinger

A Little Rock

Read the rhyme below to your children. Have them pretend to pick up a tiny "rock" from the ground. Repeat the rhyme, substituting other words such as *big, smooth* or *small, bumpy* for *tiny, little.*

I went outside
And guess what I found—
A tiny, little rock
Lying on the ground.

Elizabeth McKinnon

Rocks

Rock Family

Set out rocks in a variety of sizes. Let your children pretend the rocks are a family. Have your children name the rocks. Encourage them to make up stories about the rock family members. Let them dictate their stories into a tape recorder or to you to write down.

Pebble Counting

Prepare ten large index cards or sheets of heavy paper by numbering them with dots from 1 to 10. Put out the cards and a basket of pebbles. Let your children take turns selecting a card, placing a pebble on each dot, and counting the pebbles.

Rock Collection

Find or purchase an interesting set of rocks. (Collections of rocks can often be found at craft and hobby stores.) Place the rocks on a table along with several felt squares. Let your children take turns arranging the rocks on the felt. Encourage them to think about different ways to sort the rocks, by size, by color, by shape, or by special features. Have them explain their sorting method to you.

Hot and Cold Rocks

Explain to your children that rocks absorb and lose heat very quickly. If they are placed on a warm surface, they become warm. If they are placed somewhere cool, they become cool. Then place a rock in a warm place, such as a sunny windowsill or near a heat vent. Place another rock in the freezer or outside when it is cold. How do the rocks feel after a short time?

Rock Music

Have each of your children collect two rocks that are large enough to tap together. Show the children how to tap their rocks in rhythm. Then play some music and have the children tap their rocks for a percussion accompaniment.

Variation: Have your children collect small pebbles to put into empty yogurt containers. Tape on the lids and let the children use them as maracas.

Rocks and Water

Set out a box of rocks. Give each of your children a bowl and a small pitcher of water. Let your children select several rocks from the box and put them in their bowls. Ask them to look at the rocks and their colors. Then have them carefully pour water over their rocks. How do the rocks look now? Have the colors changed? What would happen if the rocks were dried off?

Variation: Let your children completely cover their rocks with water and observe the rocks carefully. Most rocks will have small air bubbles coming out of them.

Rocks

Pick Up the Rocks

Sung to: "Ten Little Indians"

Pick up the rocks.
Put 'em in your bucket.
Pick up the rocks.
Put 'em in your bucket.
Pick up the rocks.
Put 'em in your bucket.
Put 'em in your bucket now.

Dump all the rocks.
Dump 'em out of your bucket.
Dump all the rocks.
Dump 'em out of your bucket.
Dump all the rocks.
Dump 'em out of your bucket.
Dump 'em out of your bucket now.

Let your children pretend to pick up rocks, put them into buckets, and dump them out as you sing.

Jean Warren

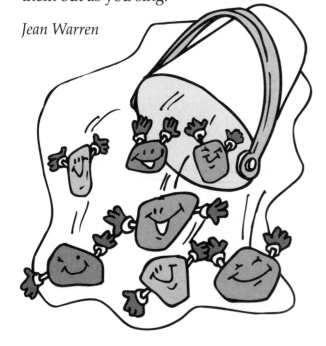

I Love Rocks

Sung to: "Three Blind Mice"

I love rocks.
I love rocks.
Big and small.
One and all.
I love rocks of every kind.
I collect whatever I find.
I wish that they all were mine.
I love rocks.

Gayle Bittinger

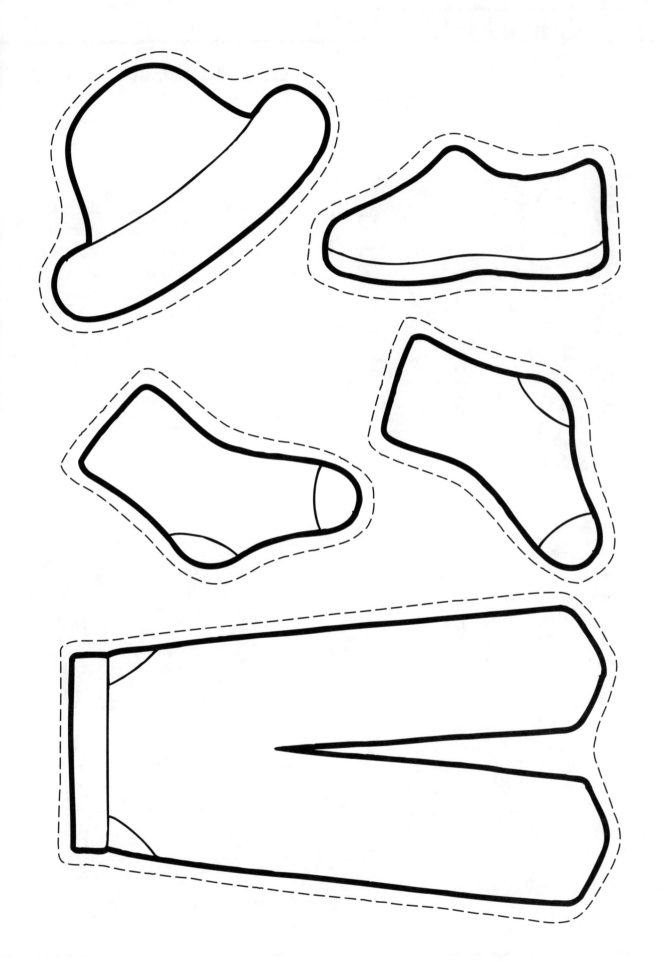

Beautiful Earth Picture

Cut 8-inch circles out of blue construction paper. Pour brown paint in a small container and put a few marbles in it. One at a time, have your children select one of the circles, place it in a box lid lined with foil, and spoon one or two of the marbles on top. Let the children gently roll the box back and forth to make an earth design. When the paint is dry, give your children small pieces of cotton to glue on their earth circles for clouds. Have them glue their circles to black construction paper "sky."

3-D Maps

Show your children a relief map. Have them feel the mountains and valleys and other land features on the map. Help your children name the different features they feel. Then give each child a shoebox lid and a handful of modeling dough. Let the children spread the dough out on the lid and use their fingers to form mountains, lakes, rivers, and valleys. If you wish, let the dough on the 3-D Maps dry and have the children paint them.

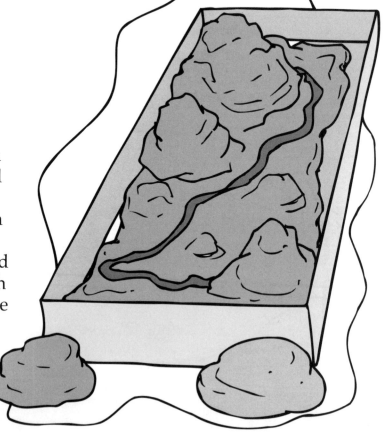

Global Language

Photocopy and cut out the game cards on page 243 and set them aside. Show your children a globe. Point out the land and the water on the globe. Show them where they live. Introduce them to some geography vocabulary such as *ocean, river, continents, islands, mountains,* and *equator.* Then mix up the game cards. Let the children take turns selecting one of the cards, naming the picture on it, and finding one like it on the globe.

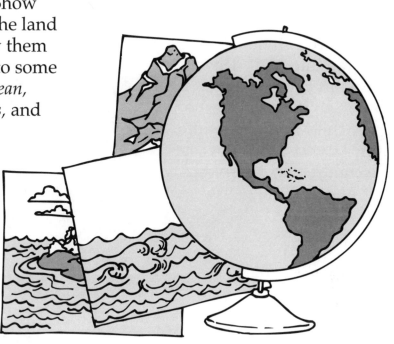

Island Hopping

Cut round island shapes out of brown construction paper. Spread them out across your room. Have your children pretend that the floor of your room is an ocean. Let them try to cross from one side of the ocean to the other by hopping from one island to another. Be sure to arrange the "islands" so there is more than one way to cross the ocean.

Our World

In the Middle

Show your children a globe. Point out the equator line that goes across the middle of the earth. Divide your children into pairs. Have one child in each pair choose an item and let the other child find the middle of it. After several items, let the children switch roles.

Small to Large

Find an outdated world map that you can cut up. Carefully cut out each of the continents. Cover the continents with clear self-stick paper for durability, if desired. Show your children the continents and tell them the names. Then let your children take turns arranging the continents in order of size from smallest to largest.

Rivers Flowing

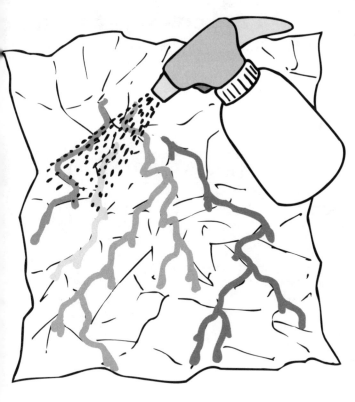

Show your children a mountain range on a globe. Have them notice that somewhere around the mountain range, there will be a river flowing from it. Explain that the snow on the mountain melts or rain falls on the mountain and flows down, often forming a river. To demonstrate this, crumple up a piece of plain white paper, then uncrumple it, and form it into a bumpy mountain shape. Draw along the ridges of the "mountain" with washable markers. Use a spray bottle to spray "rain" on the mountain. Have your children watch as the water flows down in certain places, making small rivers of color.

Volcanic Eruption

Explain to your children that many mountain ranges were formed by volcanoes, especially the ones around the Pacific Ocean. Show them the Pacific Ocean and some of the mountains on a globe. Then make a volcano with your children. Let them help you form some modeling dough into a volcano shape with an indentation in the middle. Put a spoonful of baking soda in the indentation in the volcano. Mix a little vinegar with some red food coloring. Slowly pour some of the vinegar onto the baking soda. Have your children watch as the red "lava" escapes down the sides of the volcano. Add more baking soda and vinegar as needed to keep your volcano erupting.

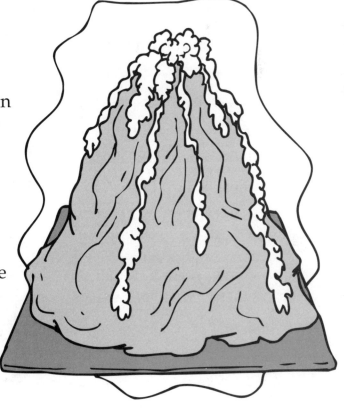

Our World

I'm Looking at a Globe

Sung to: "The Farmer in the Dell"

I'm looking at a globe,
The earth is round I see.
There's a mountain,
There's an ocean,
And there's a place for me.

Gayle Bittinger

On Our Earth

Sung to: "She'll Be Comin' Round the Mountain"

There are oceans on our earth,
Yes, there are.
There are oceans on our earth,
Yes, there are.
There are oceans on our earth,
There are oceans on our earth,
There are oceans on our earth,
Yes, there are.

Additional verses: There are mountains;
rivers; continents; volcanoes; islands.

Gayle Bittinger

Water

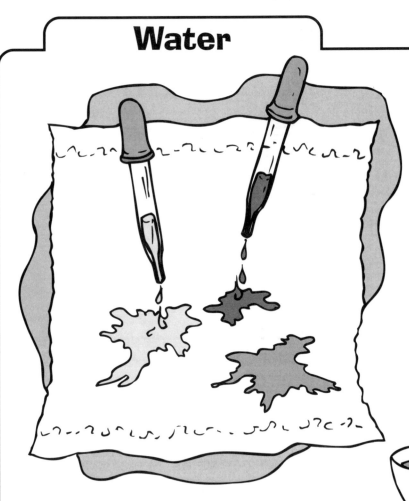

Droplet Designs

Fill several paper cups with water and add food coloring to each one. Give your children eyedroppers and paper towels. Let the children create droplet designs on their towels by using their eyedroppers to drop colored water on them. Do the towels feel wet or dry now? Have the children wait a few minutes. Now how do their towels feel? What happened to the water? (It evaporated—became warm enough to turn into a vapor and escape into the air.)

Splatter Paintings

Have your children paint designs on construction paper with different colors of tempera paint (two primary colors work well). While the paint is still wet, have the children take their papers outside. Let the children take turns using a spray bottle to squirt a little water on their paintings. Have them watch as the colors on their paintings run and mix together.

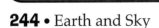

Water, Water

Photocopy the patterns on page 249. Color and cut out the child and rain cloud shapes. Tape the shapes to a nonaluminum baking sheet. Cut five raindrop shapes out of magnetic strip. Read the rhyme below out loud. Let your children take turns placing the raindrops on the child shape as the different body parts are mentioned in the rhyme.

Water, water
Everywhere,
On my face
And on my hair.
On my fingers,
On my toes.
Water, water
On my nose!

Jean Warren

Water Is a Friend of Mine

Read the poem below out loud. Let your children think of other ways they can use water.

Water is a friend of mine,
I can use it anytime.

I can spray it on the car,
I can spray it near or far.

I can play in the tub at night,
Then wash my hair clean and bright.

I can water the flowers and grass,
I can drink water from a glass.

I can jump into a pool,
And swim in water clean and cool.

I can play when the rain comes down,
Making puddles all around.

Water is a friend of mine,
I can use it anytime.

Jean Warren

Water

Which Holds the Most?

Show your children five empty containers that hold varying amounts of water. Ask them to estimate which container holds the most water, the next most, and so on. Line up the containers in the order of their estimations from most to least. Then let your children count as you pour cups of water into one of the containers until it is full. Write the number of cups on a paper cup and place it in front of that container. Repeat with the other four containers. Ask your children if the containers are arranged in the correct order from most to least water volume or if some need to be moved. Have the children help rearrange the containers as necessary.

More or Less

Collect several 8-ounce containers, such as a baby bottle, a short glass, a tall glass, a bowl, etc. It is important that each container holds exactly 8 ounces. Show your children a measuring cup that has ounce markings on the sides. Show them where 8 ounces is and mark it with colored tape. Ask the children to estimate which containers they think the water will fit in. Pour the water into one of those containers. Then ask the children if they think any of the other containers are the same volume. Let the children watch as you pour 8 ounces of water into each of the other containers.

Water Exploration

Spread towels on a low table and place several dishpans filled partway with water on top of them. Collect a variety of small plastic containers such as margarine tubs or yogurt containers. Use a nail to punch various numbers and sizes of holes in the bottoms of the containers. Give your children the plastic containers and let them experiment with pouring and measuring the water in the dishpans. Encourage the children to observe, discuss, and explore what happens with the different containers.

Water Snacks

Take advantage of snacktime to demonstrate and discuss what happens when water is boiled, frozen, evaporated, and used to dilute. For example, boil water to make noodles or hard-boiled eggs; freeze water to make frozen pops or ice cubes with fruit pieces inside; dry fruits to demonstrate evaporation; dilute juice concentrate to make fruit juice.

Water

Water Song

Sung to: "The Wheels on the Bus"

Water is wet and it pours like this,
Pours like this, pours like this.
Water is wet and it pours like this,
See how it goes.

Water is liquid and it sprinkles like this,
Sprinkles like this, sprinkles like this.
Water is liquid and it sprinkles like this,
See how it goes.

Water is clear and it bubbles like this,
Bubbles like this, bubbles like this.
Water is clear and it bubbles like this,
See how it goes.

Let your children pour water, sprinkle water, and make bubbles in water while you sing this song together.

Gayle Bittinger

Splash, Splash, Splash

Sung to: "The Wheels on the Bus"

Oh, the water in the cup goes
Splash, splash, splash,
Splash, splash, splash,
Splash, splash, splash.
Oh, the water in the cup goes
Splash, splash, splash
When I pour it out.

Additional verses: Oh, the water in the bottle goes squirt, squirt, squirt when I squeeze it out; Oh, the water in the sponge goes drip, drip, drip when I squish it out.

Jean Warren

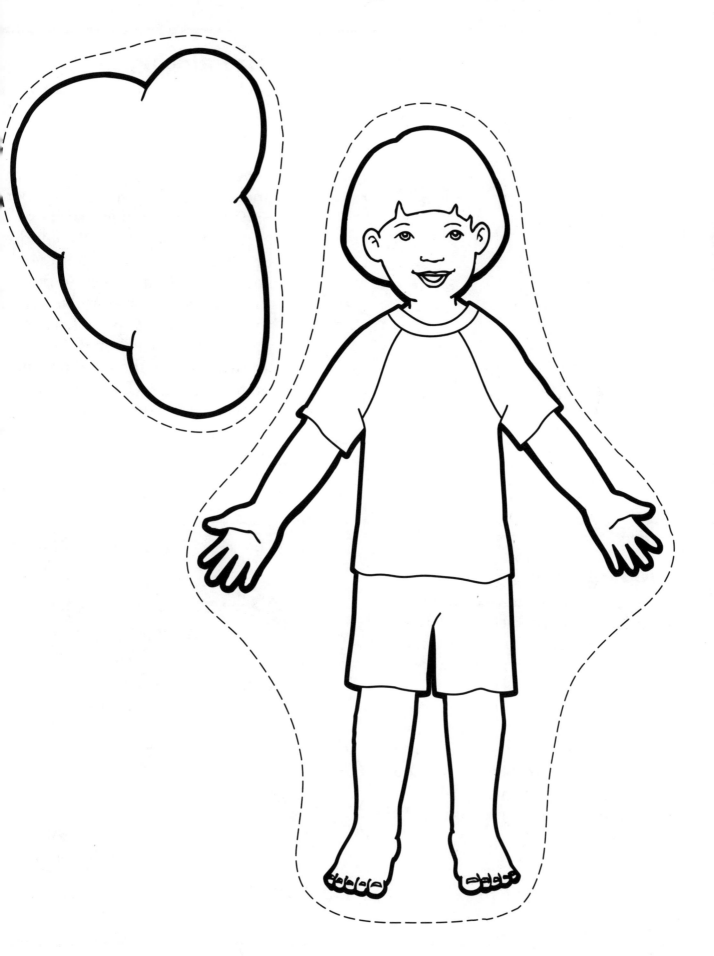

Air

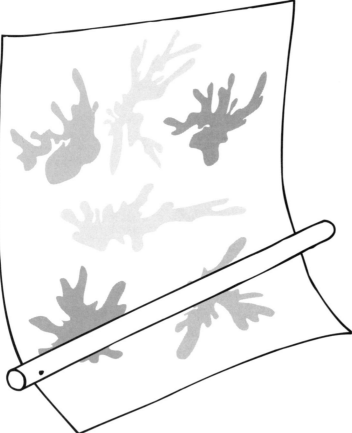

Air Painting

Collect a plastic drinking straw for each of your children. Use a straight pin to poke one or two holes near one end of each straw. Give each child one of the straws and a piece of construction paper. Spoon a little tempera paint on each child's paper. Let the children practice blowing air out of their straws. Encourage them to put their hands in front of their straws to feel the air coming out. Then have them blow through their straws to move the paint around on their papers. (The holes in the straws help prevent the paint from being inhaled in case a child breathes in instead of out.)

Moving Air

Cut fan shapes out of cardboard and attach craft-stick handles. Let your children decorate the fans as desired with crayons, markers, or stickers. Place objects of varying weight on a table (feathers, cotton balls, toy cars, blocks, etc.). Have your children use their fans to try to make the objects move without touching them. Which objects moved? Which objects did not?

Air Takes Up Space

Fill a clear bowl with water. Set out the bowl along with a tall clear glass and a paper napkin. Ask one of your children to crumple the paper napkin and place it in the bottom of the tall clear glass. Have the children observe while you turn the glass upside down and, keeping it level, lower it into the bowl of water. What is happening in the glass? Why isn't the water going into the glass? Lift the glass out of the water and take out the napkin. Why is it dry? (The glass was filled with air, so there was no room for the water to get it.)

Experiments With Air

Give each of your children a cotton ball, a plastic drinking straw, and a paper scrap. Let the children experiment with the items to answer the following questions: "Can you feel air? (Blow air through the straw onto your hand.) Can you make a cotton ball move without touching it? (Blow on it.) Can you pick up a small piece of paper with the straw? (Hold the straw against the paper and suck on the straw.) What other experiments can you think up?"

Air

Catching Air

Place an old bed sheet on the floor. Have your children hold onto the edges of the sheet. Tell them that they are going to use the sheet to "catch" some air. Then have them lift up the sheet and quickly bring it down. The middle of the sheet arches up because air is caught underneath it. Have the children see how much air they can catch by moving the sheet in different ways, such as slowly, quickly, up high, down low, etc.

Paper Drop

Show your children two identical pieces of paper. Crumple one piece and leave the other one flat. Have the children predict which sheet of paper will hit the floor first when you drop them from the same height. Then drop the papers. The crumpled piece of paper landed first because it had less surface area to trap air and slow its descent. Then give your children pieces of paper and let them experiment. Encourage them to try dropping papers different heights, papers crumpled different amounts, etc.

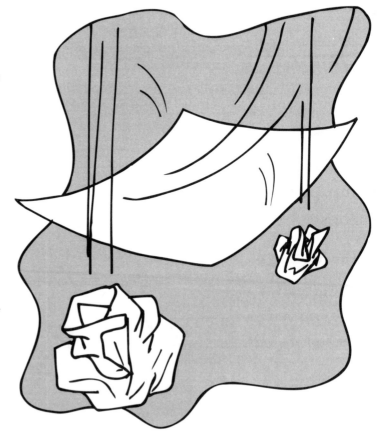

Surprise!

Use the patterns on page 255 to cut the following shapes out of felt: blue riding horse, yellow duck, red puppy, and green alligator. Place the shapes in front of a flannelboard. Read the rhyme below to your children. Put each shape on the flannelboard as it is mentioned in the rhyme.

I found a box of silly toys.

They really weren't much fun.

They just kind of laid there,

Every single one.

I ran and got my air pump

To see what it could do.

Pump, pump, pump, pump,

Surprise! A riding horse that's blue.

Next, I pulled out of the box

A funny sort of fellow.

Pump, pump, pump, pump,

Surprise! A duck of sunny yellow.

Reaching in again, I found

A flat body and a head.

Pump, pump, pump, pump,

Surprise! A puppy that was red.

In the bottom of the box I found

Something long and mean.

Pump, pump, pump, pump,

Surprise! An alligator colored green.

Jean Warren

Variation: Find four inflatable pool toys. Substitute the names and colors of those toys for the ones in the rhyme. Have another adult inflate each toy as you read about it in the rhyme.

Extension: Give each of your children an inflatable toy to experiment with putting air in it and taking air out.

Air on My Face

Find or purchase a battery-operated hand-held fan. Show the fan to your children and let them feel the moving air against their hands or faces. Now have them sit in a circle and close their eyes. Slowly walk around the inside of the circle, letting the fan blow air on the children's faces. Have them make a fanning motion with their hands when they feel the air blowing on their faces.

Air

It Is Air

Sung to: "Frère Jacques"

You can't see it, you can't see it,
But it's there, everywhere.
It fills up balloons,
It takes up space.
It is air, it is air.

You can't see it, you can't see it,
But it's there, everywhere.
It makes things move
When it blows.
It is air, it is air.

You can't see it, you can't see it,
But it's there, everywhere.
It makes loud noises
As it rushes by us.
It is air, it is air.

Gayle Bittinger

Air Is All Around Me

Sung to: "If You're Happy and You Know It"

Oh, the air is all around me,
This I know.
It can push me
When it really wants to blow.
It can dry my clothes and hair,
It can blow things everywhere.
Oh, the air is all around me,
This I know.

Oh, the air is all around me,
This I know.
It can move super fast
Or super slow.
It can help me play a tune,
It can raise a big balloon.
Oh, the air is all around me,
This I know.

Jean Warren

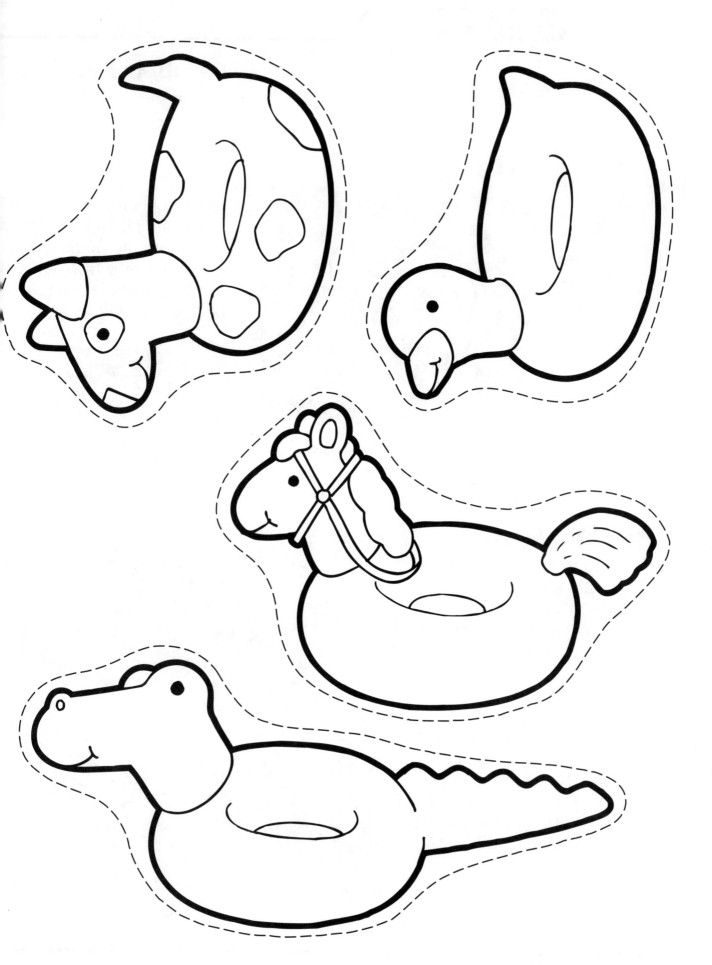

Rainbow

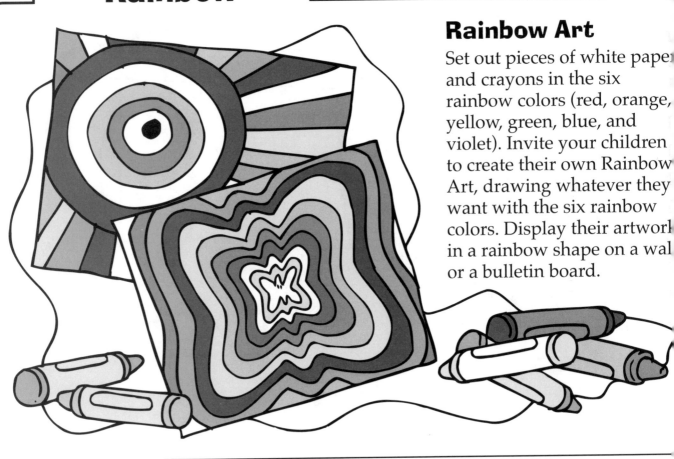

Rainbow Art

Set out pieces of white paper and crayons in the six rainbow colors (red, orange, yellow, green, blue, and violet). Invite your children to create their own Rainbow Art, drawing whatever they want with the six rainbow colors. Display their artwork in a rainbow shape on a wall or a bulletin board.

Rainbow Mural

Cut red, orange, yellow, green, blue, and violet construction paper into 2-inch-by-9-inch strips. Set out the paper strips and tape or glue. Let your children make paper chains with the loops, making a separate chain for each color. When you have long chains for each color, hang them up in rainbow arcs on a wall or a bulletin board, starting with red and working down with orange, yellow, green, blue, and violet.

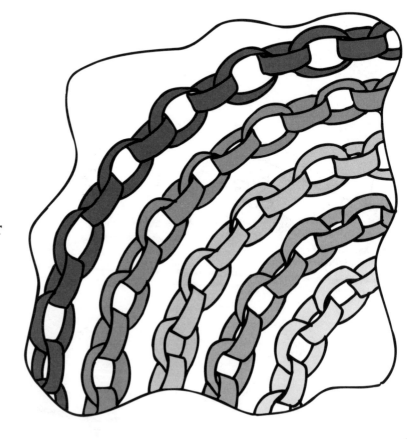

A Rainbow

Let your children fill in the blanks as you read the story below out loud.

I see a rainbow.

It is more colorful than _____.

My favorite rainbow color is _____.

If I look under the rainbow, I will find _____.

To catch a rainbow, I will _____.

I can use my rainbow to _____.

If I had two rainbows, I would give one to _____.

Jean Warren

Cooperation Game

Let your children work together to create this rainbow on the floor. Ask your children to look around the room, collect all the red objects they can find, and put the objects in a pile. Repeat with the remaining five rainbow colors (orange, yellow, green, blue, and violet). Then let your children arrange the objects on the floor in a rainbow shape. First have them put all the red objects in a big arc, then the yellow objects under them, and so on, until the rainbow is completed. Let your children stand back and admire their rainbow before putting the objects away.

Rainbow

Dough Rainbow

Make a batch of modeling dough by mixing together 2 cups flour, 1 cup salt, ¾ cup water, and 2 tablespoons vegetable oil. Add more flour or water as needed to reach the right consistency. Divide the dough into six equal parts. Use a small amount of tempera paint or food coloring to color each part of the dough a different color of the rainbow (red, orange, yellow, green, blue, and violet). Let your children take turns rolling out each color of dough into a "snake" and then curving it into an arc. Help them arrange the arcs to make a rainbow. Talk about the colors in the rainbow.

Rainbow Surprise

Make this special gelatin treat with your children. Coat a clear, heat-tempered (such as Pyrex brand) bowl with nonstick cooking spray. In a separate bowl, prepare a small package of gelatin. Pour it into the prepared bowl. Once it is set, repeat with another color of gelatin. Continue until you have as many layers as you wish. Serve each child a spoonful of Rainbow Surprise in a bowl. Which flavor tastes the best?

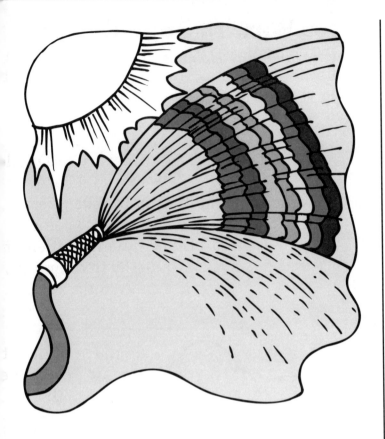

Rainbows Outside

On a sunny day, use a garden hose to spray a fine mist of water across the sun's rays. Have your children stand with their backs to the sun and look for a rainbow in the mist. Name the six rainbow colors with your children (red, orange, yellow, green, blue, and violet). Explain that sunlight contains all these colors mixed together, and when it hits the water from the garden hose (or raindrops in the sky), all the colors are separated and form a rainbow.

Note: Scientifically speaking, a rainbow is made up of seven colors—red, orange, yellow, green, blue, indigo, and violet—that always appear in the same order. Because the color indigo is very difficult to distinguish between blue and violet, it has been left out of the activities in this section.

Felt Rainbow

Using the pattern on page 261, cut rainbow arcs out of the appropriate colors of felt. Let your children take turns arranging the arcs on a flannelboard while you sing the song below together. Talk about the order of the colors when you are finished.

Sung to: "The Bear Went Over the Mountain"

We're making up a rainbow,
We're making up a rainbow,
We're making up a rainbow,
For everyone to see.

The first color is red,
The first color is red,
The first color is red,
For everyone to see.

Additional verses: The second color is orange; The third color is yellow; The fourth color is green; The fifth color is blue; The sixth color is violet.

Kathie Vogel

Rainbow

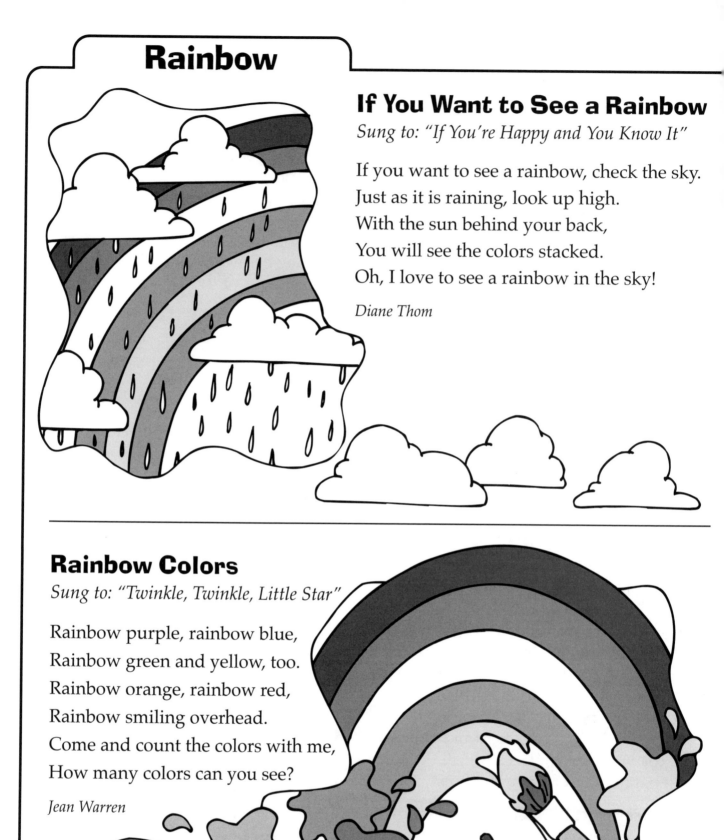

If You Want to See a Rainbow

Sung to: "If You're Happy and You Know It"

If you want to see a rainbow, check the sky.
Just as it is raining, look up high.
With the sun behind your back,
You will see the colors stacked.
Oh, I love to see a rainbow in the sky!

Diane Thom

Rainbow Colors

Sung to: "Twinkle, Twinkle, Little Star"

Rainbow purple, rainbow blue,
Rainbow green and yellow, too.
Rainbow orange, rainbow red,
Rainbow smiling overhead.
Come and count the colors with me,
How many colors can you see?

Jean Warren

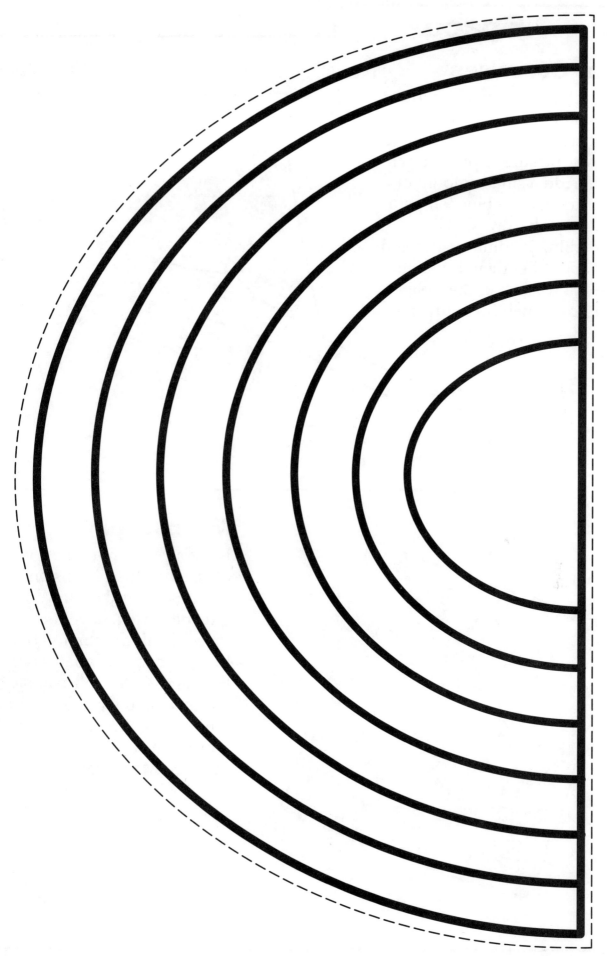

Space

Star Surprises

For each of your children, draw star shapes on a piece of white construction paper with a white crayon. (Be sure to press down hard.) Add a small amount of water to black or blue tempera paint to make a wash. Give your children paintbrushes and the papers. Let them brush the tempera wash over their papers to discover their Star Surprises.

Moonscapes

Let your children glue a variety of sizes of dried beans on squares of cardboard. When the glue has dried, have them lay pieces of aluminum foil on top o their cardboard squares and fold the edges of the foil around the backs of their squares. Then hav them gently press the foil down around the beans to create textured Moonscapes.

Four Little Stars

Use the patterns on pages 268 and 269 as guides for cutting four star shapes out of white felt, a moon shape and a comet shape out of yellow felt, and a spaceship and a satellite shape out of gray felt. Cut a big cloud shape out of black felt as well. Use the shapes on a flannelboard to dramatize the actions as you read the poem below.

Four little stars on a cold winter's night,
Twinkled and twinkled ever so bright.
One saw a comet and shot away,
Three little stars now twinkle that way.

Three little stars on a cold winter's night,
Twinkled and twinkled ever so bright.
One saw a spaceship and shot away,
Two little stars now twinkle that way.

Two little stars on a cold winter's night,
Twinkled and twinkled ever so bright.
One saw a satellite and shot away,
One little star now twinkles that way.

One little star on a cold winter's night,
Twinkled and twinkled ever so bright.
It saw the moon and shot away,
No little stars now twinkle that way.

"Where, oh, where did the little stars
    go?"
I asked the comet. Did it know?
But the comet didn't know where the
    stars had gone,
So I asked the spaceship when it came
    along.

But the spaceship said it just didn't
    know,
Where those four little stars did go.
So I asked the satellite up in the sky,
But it just beeped as it flew by.

Where, oh, where did those little stars
    go?
Surely the moon would have to know.
"Bright yellow moon, oh, can you say,
Where are the stars that shot away?"

The moon just smiled and winked
    at me,
"The stars didn't go, as you'll soon see!"
And sure enough, when the wind did
    blow,
A big black cloud started to go.
Then out popped the stars, gone no
    more—
One, two, three, and four.

Jean Warren

Space

Star Experiment

Tell your children that the stars are always shining in the sky. Do they believe you? What can't we see the stars in the daytime? Ask your children to help you do this experiment to show them why. Turn on all the lights in your room. Have two or three children stand away from the group and give each one a "star" (a flashlight that's been turned on). Ask the group if they can see the light from the flashlights. (Not very well.) This is like the daytime. The stars are shining, but we can't see them. Gradually darken the room. What happens to the light coming from the "stars?" Is it easier or harder to see? Help the children understand that just as they can't see the light from the flashlights when the room lights are on, they can't see the light from the stars when the sun is shining.

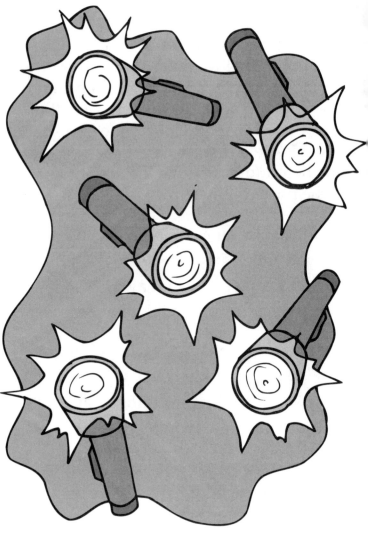

Star Scopes

Give each of your children a 4-inch cardboard tube with a black paper circle taped on one end. Let the children gently punch holes in the paper-covered ends of their tubes with toothpicks. Have the children hold their tubes up to the light while looking through the uncovered ends. The light will shine through the holes, creating miniature planetariums.

Space Experiments

Explain to your children that most astronauts are scientists and are trained to conduct experiments in space. Let the children pretend that they are astronauts as they do the experiments below.

Weighing Moon Rocks—Give your children some "moon" rocks (any ordinary rocks will do). Show them how to use a small scale to weigh their rocks. (A bathroom scale with large numbers works great.)

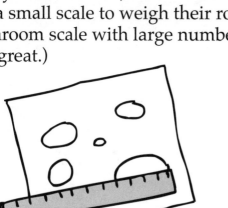

Measuring Moon Rocks—Have your children place their moon rocks on pieces of paper and trace around them with markers. Then show the children how to measure the rock tracings with a ruler. Help them label each tracing with its largest measurement.

Testing Gravity—Explain that the earth has gravity and pulls everything towards it. Let your children throw balls into the air and see if they fall down to the earth or if they float in the air. The balls fall down to the earth because the earth's gravity pulls them back. Explain that in space there is no gravity, so everything floats. Have them imagine what it would be like to have everything around them float—clothes, toys, books, food. How would life in space be different?

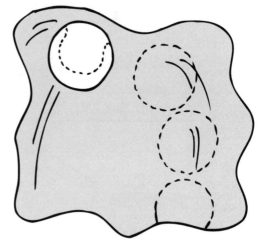

Moving in Space—Astronauts who want to work in one place and not float around must strap their bodies in place. Let your children pretend to experiment with weightlessness in a spaceship. Have them pretend to float from one area of the spaceship to another, strapping their bodies in each time.

Space

Star Sort

Cut several sizes of stars out of yellow construction paper. (Enlarge the star pattern on page 268 to use as a guide, if you wish.) Let your children arrange them in order from smallest to largest. Then have them count the stars.

Star Colors

Cut a star out of posterboard and color each of its five points a different color. Color the ends of five clothespins to match the colors on the star points. To play the game, have your children clip each clothespin on the matching colored star point.

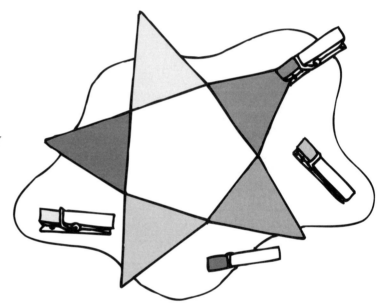

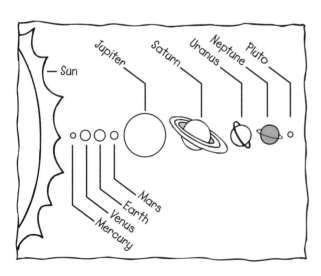

Planet Sizes

Cut out felt circles in various sizes to represent the planets and sun in our solar system. Place the planets on a flannelboard in the proper order. (See illustration.) Discuss the sizes of the earth, other planets, and the sun with your children. Then let the children arrange the planets and the sun in a line from the largest to the smallest.

Little Stars

Sung to: "Twinkle, Twinkle, Little Star"

Twinkle, twinkle, little stars,
Friends of Jupiter and Mars.
All you do the whole night through
Is twinkle, twinkle, twinkle, too.
Twinkle, twinkle, little stars,
Friends of Jupiter and Mars.

Jean Warren

Nine Little Planets

Sung to: "Ten Little Indians"

Let's sing about out solar system,
Let's sing about out solar system,
Let's sing about out solar system,
Nine little planets and a sun.

One little, two little, three little planets,
Four little, five little, six little planets,
Seven little, eight little, nine little planets,
And our great big sun.

Round and round go the planets,
Round and round go the planets,
Round and round go the planets,
Round our great big sun.

Jean Warren

Moon Glow

Sung to: "Twinkle, Twinkle, Little Star"

Moon glow, moon glow in the night.
Moon glow, moon glow, gentle light.
How I love to see you there,
Softly shining everywhere.
Moon glow, moon glow in the night.
Moon glow, moon glow, gentle light.

Margaret Timmons

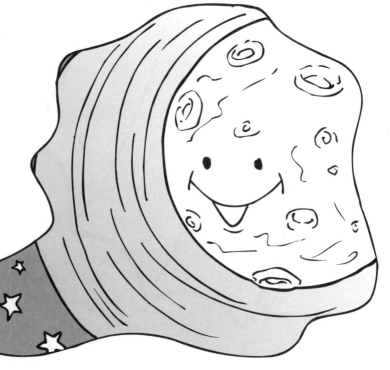

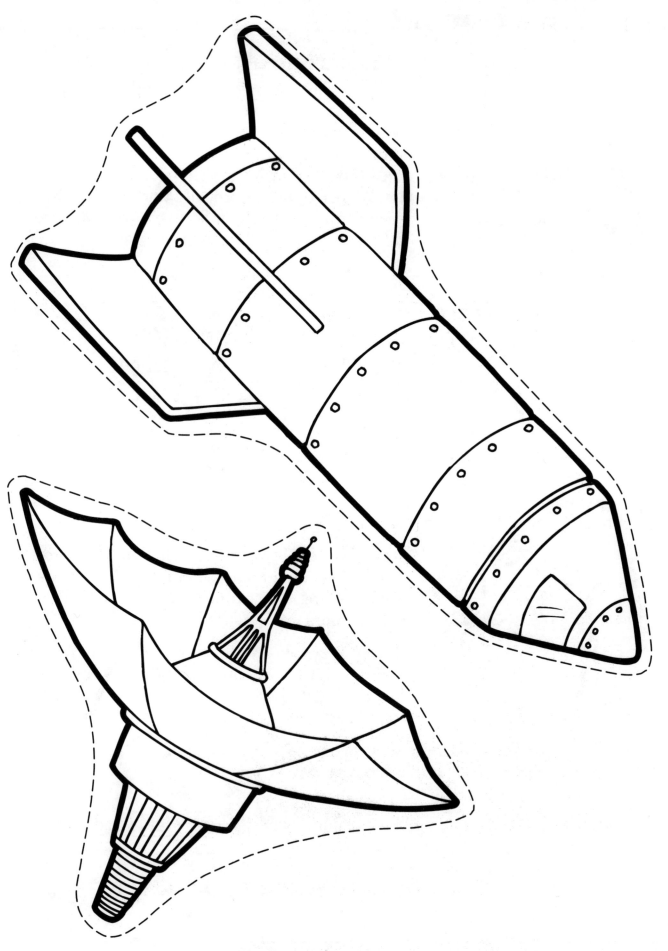

Environment

Nature Mural

Go on a walk with your children. Let them collect small nature objects such as feathers, flowers, leaves, and grass in small paper bags. When you return, let the children weave their objects through the holes in a fishing net. Encourage them to weave items horizontally, vertically, and diagonally. Hang the net on a wall or a bulletin board. Continue to add objects as the children find them.

Displaying Nature

Let your children bring in nature items from home, and give them many opportunities to collect them. Use their collections to create nature displays throughout your room. Here are a few ideas for you and your children to try together.

Display Strips—Attach bulletin board strips made out of corkboard to your walls. Use push pins to hang your children's collections of lightweight, two-dimensional items.

Jump Rope Display—Stretch a multi-colored jump rope between two poles, along a wall, or across a door opening. Use clothespins to hang lightweight nature items from the rope.

Sheet Display—Make a simple display with a white or light-colored flat bed sheet. Arrange the sheet on the floor or on a table. Place your children's collections on the sheet to highlight them.

Three-Dimensional Art Display—Fasten small cardboard boxes to bulletin boards to display collections of small items.

Display Shelves—Designate two or three special shelves for your children's collections. If you wish, have the children help you paint these shelves a bright color. Let them arrange their collections on the shelves.

Art With Recyclables

Have your children and their families collect items that might ordinarily be thrown away, such as plastic containers and lids, packaging materials, cardboard boxes and containers, fabric and yarn scraps, and junk mail. Set out the items along with staplers, tape, and glue. Let your children use the recyclable materials any way they wish to create their own sculptures or other kind of art. Encourage them to arrange and fasten the materials together with the glue, tape, and staples.

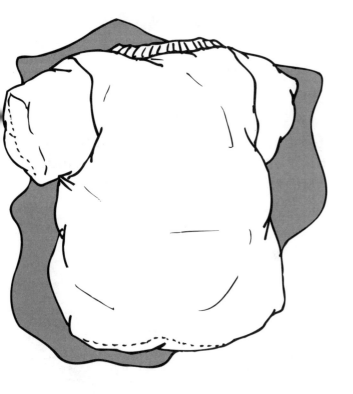

T-Shirt Pillows

Collect old sheets and towels and anything else that could be used for stuffing pillows. When you have several bags full of stuffing, ask each of your children to bring in an old, clean T-shirt. (Or, buy inexpensive shirts at a secondhand store or garage sale.) Sew or tie the arms and necks closed. Let your children help you tear the sheets and towels into strips. Show them how to stuff the fabric strips into their T-shirts to make pillows. Sew or tie the bottom of the shirts closed. Let your children use their T-Shirt Pillows in your library corner or take them home.

Environment

What Can I Do With This?

Explain to your children that we throw away a lot of garbage. One of the ways to take care of our earth includes finding ways to make less garbage. One of the ways we can decrease the amount of garbage we make is to use objects over and over again instead of throwing them away. Hold up an object that would usually end up in the garbage. Ask your children to think of other things they could do with it. Let them continue their brainstorming with other throwaway objects.

Cleanup Day

Organize a Cleanup Day with your children. Photocopy the Cleanup Day Invitation on page 280. Fill in the information and make copies for each of your children to decorate and take home. Have them give the invitations to friends and families to encourage them to gather together to clean and spruce up a favorite outdoor area. Have available plenty of garbage bags for collecting litter and recyclables and a variety of outdoor tools for gardening and yard work. Set aside an area for a garden and give each child a small flower or shrub to plant in it.

Save a Tree

Explain to your children that recycling a 3-foot stack of newspaper will save one tree from being cut down and turned into paper. Then put a piece of masking tape 3 feet up on a wall in your room. Have the children bring in newspaper and stack them in a pile under the tape. Each time a 3-foot stack is collected, take the stack to the recycling center and put a mark on a tree-shaped chart. At the end of a month or another specified time, count how many trees your children have saved. Then celebrate by going outside and having a picnic under a tree!

Recycling Baskets

Set out two wastebaskets in your room. Tape a piece of construction paper and other examples of paper that can be recycled to one of the wastebaskets. To the other basket, tape a napkin, a facial tissue, and other samples of nonrecyclable paper and garbage. Then talk with your children about recycling and its benefits. Discuss the two wastebaskets with your children. Set out several examples of recyclable paper and nonrecyclable garbage and let the children put them into the appropriate cans. Encourage the children to ask you if they have any questions about what is recyclable and what is not.

Environment

Nature Walk

Take this special nature walk to help your children truly see the wonders of nature and to learn to look closely at the world around them. A day or two before your outing, walk the trail yourself. Watch for hazards such as low hanging branches or prickly bushes. Make sure the planned route is not too difficult for your children. You may spot a bird's nest or an animal's burrow that you can point out to the children during the walk. Try including some or all of the activities described below before, during, and after your Nature Walk.

Treasure Collectors—Before the walk, have your children make containers to hold the treasures they will find along the way. Let them decorate brown paper bags with nature stickers. Or, have them add pipe cleaner handles to the bottom halves of cardboard milk cartons.

Color Comparisons—Cut small squares of several different colors of construction paper. Hand them out to your children and have them try to find nature items of the same color.

Nature Paint—If you are lucky enough to find a berry patch, collect some of the fruit to make Nature Paint. Crush the berries with a wooden spoon and add a drop or two of vinegar to prevent mold. Let the children use craft sticks to spread the paint on sheets of construction paper. (Be sure the children's clothing is covered when using a natural dye like this.)

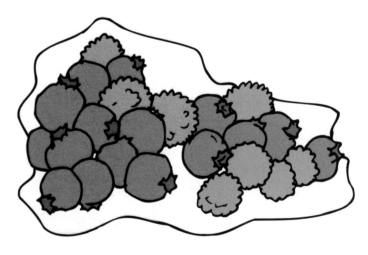

Earth Day

April 22 is Earth Day. People across the country celebrate this day by wearing green, planting trees, and learning how to use resources wisely. As you discuss Earth Day with your children, have them name some activities they would like to do, such as turning off the lights, planting flower seeds, wearing green, or recycling paper and aluminum cans. Each day, let them tell you what they did to take care of the earth.

Earth Day Badges

Cut circles out of heavy paper. Set out the circles, green and blue paint, paintbrushes, and glitter. Let your children paint designs on the circles. Then have them sprinkle a small amount of glitter over the paint. Allow the paint to dry. Punch a hole in each circle and hang it from a piece of yarn. Let your children wear their Earth Day Badges as they sing the song below.

Sung to: "Yankee Doodle"

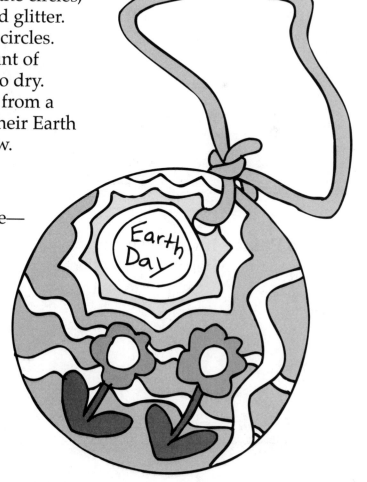

I'm proud to wear my Earth Day Badge—
I give the earth a hand.
I pick up litter, care for trees,
Recycle what I can.
I'm an Earth Day helper
Each and every day.
I take care of Mother Earth
In, oh, so many ways.

Gayle Bittinger

Environment

Stomp and Pitch

Collect three to five empty, uncrushed aluminum cans for each of your children. Set out the cans in a row, and place several boxes about 3 feet away. Have your children smash the cans as flat as possible and pitch the flattened cans into the boxes. Stomping and pitching are great ways for children to exercise their strength and large motor skills. Recycle the cans when you are finished. If you wish, sing the song below while they stomp and pitch.

Sung to: "Paw, Paw Patch"

Stompin' on cans and throwin' them in
    the box,

Stompin' on cans and throwin' them
    in the box,

Stompin' on cans and throwin'
    them in the box,

Way down yonder in the
    recycle patch.

Jean Warren

Earth Day Charades

Copy the game cards on page 279. Select two or three children to stand up. Show them one of the cards. Let them all pretend to do the activity shown on the card. Show all of the cards to the other children. Have them pick the card that shows the activity the children are acting out. Repeat for the remaining cards.

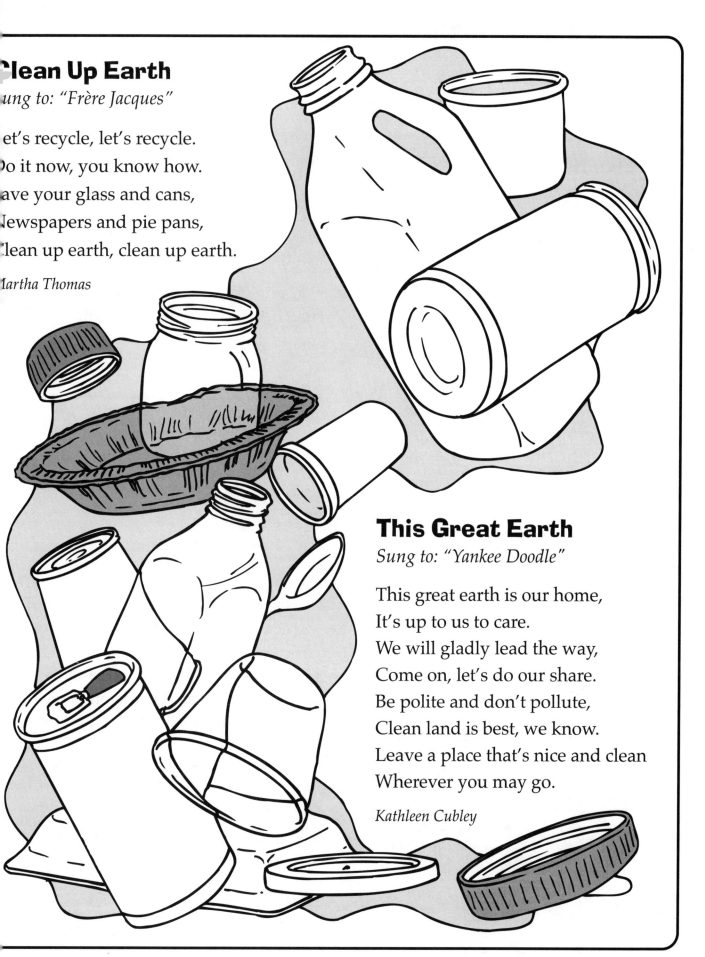

Clean Up Earth

Sung to: "Frère Jacques"

Let's recycle, let's recycle.
Do it now, you know how.
Save your glass and cans,
Newspapers and pie pans,
Clean up earth, clean up earth.

Martha Thomas

This Great Earth

Sung to: "Yankee Doodle"

This great earth is our home,
It's up to us to care.
We will gladly lead the way,
Come on, let's do our share.
Be polite and don't pollute,
Clean land is best, we know.
Leave a place that's nice and clean
Wherever you may go.

Kathleen Cubley

Environment

Nature's Partner

Sung to: "Do Your Ears Hang Low?"

Do you pull out weeds?
Do you plant a lot of seeds?
Do you water all your plants,
And give them all the care
 they need?
Then you really are a gardener,
You're nature's favorite partner.
Do you plant some seeds?

Diane Thom

Down at the Dump

Sung to: "Down by the Station"

Down at the dump early in the morning,
See the dump trucks standing in a row.
See them dump the garbage
In a great big pile,
Dump, dump, dump, dump,
Watch them go.

Pretty soon our dumps will all be full,
We had better figure out something to do.
We could all recycle
Some of our garbage,
Recycle, recycle,
Watch us go.

Out in the garden, we could make a pile
Of our food scraps so they can decay.
See us dump the scraps
In a great big pile,
Dump, dump, dump, dump,
Watch us go.

Then we could send off all our cans and jars
So they can be used to make some new ones.
See us dump the cans and jars
In a great big bag,
Dump, dump, dump, dump,
Watch us go.

Let's all recycle, let's all give a hand,
'Cause if we recycle, we'll have a nicer land.
See us sorting out
All of our garbage,
Sort, sort, sort, sort,
Watch us go.

Jean Warren

Cleanup Day
Invitation

Who: _____

Where: _____

What: _____

When: _____

Please join us!